Desktop Production Standards

SECOND EDITION

Bonus Section: Contract Standards
Also Includes: Web Production Times

by
Robert C. Brenner, MSEE, MSSM

BRENNER INFORMATION GROUP
P.O. Box 721000
San Diego, CA 92172-1000
(619) 538-0093

Desktop Production Standards
Second Edition

Printed in the United States of America

ISBN 0-929535-19-7

Published by
BRENNER INFORMATION GROUP
P.O. Box 721000
San Diego, CA 92172-1000
(619) 538-0093
www.brennerbooks.com
info@brennerbooks.com

Table of Contents

Desktop Production Standards

I. Introduction

"Until you measure, you can't control." - Roger Dickeson

Desktop production standards provide timing baselines for producing usable (and billable) output on desktop computer systems. Desktop production standards specifically involve machines and machine operators.

Machine standards are performance benchmarks unique to the system configuration being used to produce work. They specify time limitations (or advantages) specific to the hardware and software applied to a job. The times to produce a laser printed image or to scan a graphic-heavy transparency are directly related to the speed at which the computer's input/output bus sends or receives data, the speed of the peripheral devices that process digital data, the speed of the interface cable and the speed at which an application program can translate human intent into digital output.

Operator standards refer to the physical time in which an average individual can produce an acceptable document on paper, film, or some other information media using a "typical" system. Thus, if the "standard" desktop configuration is a 100 MHz PC with 16 MB of RAM, a 750 MB hard disk connected to an 8 ppm 600 dpi laser printer and a 1-minute-per-square inch scanner, then all timing parameters are normalized to this criteria.

This special report was produced to clarify what is normal in production. It is also intended to illuminate "holes" in your operation and to expose those places where technology, training and process restructure can enhance the flow of work and make your business more profitable.

Standards become reference points from which to measure and evaluate. You cannot begin to price, or to estimate a job until you know how long it takes to complete each portion of the project. Without agreed standards of performance, you and your customer may disagree on what was expected. This reference book will take you methodically through time standards (machine and operator) and how they can be applied to the services that you provide.

As an added bonus, this report includes performance contracts and standard terms and conditions used in the industry today. Contract standards define what is acceptable in your industry. They establish an agreement between buyer and seller by clearly describing specifically how and when production will occur, the criteria for acceptance of the work and how payment will be made.

Work contracts exist in many forms—"customer agreements," "terms and conditions," "standard trade practices," and "fine print." They establish a common reference for buyer and seller, and they minimize confusion and conflict in business transactions. Every point of contention should be addressed and resolved before you to expend billable hours on a job. You want each job clearly described to avoid resolution by litigation. If either party to a transaction acts contrary to what was agreed upon in advance, then the other party is being denied due process and is being injured by the performance (or lack of) by the other. The clearer you can define the rules, the less chance for confusion, mistrust or legal hostility. This is why contract standards have been included in this report.

Part I describes how this reference book came into being. It explains how to use the information in this report to generate your own budgeted hourly rates so you can quote a flat rate on your next job.

Part II provides tables of machine standards. The values listed in the tables are based on our own surveys and research into hardware and software performance benchmarks.

This section also shows you how to establish your own machine standards—benchmarks that are unique to the hardware and software that you are currently using. After providing examples for each, blank worksheets are provided for your use. The software disk that came with this reference book also contains spreadsheets that you can use to perform this part of your standards analysis. Updating your machine standards is easy once you've developed your own baselines.

Part III addresses operator performance standards. After defining what these are, this section provides tabular data covering input processes, creative design, page layout and output processes such as laser printing, imagesetting, film recording, CD-ROM and more.

The information provided in the tables was derived from our own surveys. In Part III, we also compare our standards with the standards of several other organizations. Operator standards include time to design and time to layout documents. Design performance is partitioned into graphic design, logo design and logotype. Desktop page layout is partitioned into specific product categories: announcements, book covers, book interior pages, brochures, flyers, newsletters, and much more.

This section also includes worksheets to help you establish your own operator production times. Each job can be partitioned into tasks. Each task takes a finite amount of time to perform based on the hardware and software used and on the individual performing the work. On some days a person will have better productivity than on others. But, generally, operator performance time should be near the average that you establish. One thing that can affect performance time is how often an operator has performed a task. Desktop system operators get faster with experience. Therefore, we've included in this section a way to determine a learning curve for each function. By knowing where a person is on the learning curve, you can determine their value to the organization and the pay level that is warranted.

Part IV shows you how to use machine and operator standards to develop baseline budgeted hourly rates (BHRs). BHRs are cost estimates. They show you what it costs to produce any output of service or product. You add your profit and return on investment to a BHR to produce a price that you can quote for a particular service. Then you set your actual price at what the market will bear. Thus, if page layout has an associated BHR of $23 an hour based on 30% productivity, and you want to earn 10% profit and 12% return on investment for each job, the price that you quote will be $28.06 an hour ($23 plus $2.30 profit plus $2.76 ROI = $28.06) or higher depending on the marketplace. Ample worksheets are provided to help you generate your own BHRs.

Finally, Part V covers contract or agreement standards. The examples contained in this section become a shopping list to help you develop your own set of custom standards that you can use when dealing with customers. The information contained in Part V was gleaned from actual contracts and Terms & Conditions (T&C) currently used in the desktop services industry. This is how the successful shops define performance. This information is provided to prevent trouble while increasing your potential for maximum profit.

Part VI is a glossary of terms and expressions used in this book. These definitions establish a common reference point from which to evaluate each of the desktop services that you'll find addressed in the tabular examples.

How The Data Was Collected

During a recent meeting of the Publishers Marketing Association, I was approached by the president of a successful book publishing company. He was holding a copy of one of our pricing reference books. This entrepreneur pointed out that our pricing tables gave both the price per page and price per hour for interior book layout. He showed me a page from the pricing tables and asked if he could divide the price per page by the dollars per hour and get hours per page. He would then use this as a rough measure of how long it takes a typical computer operator to lay out a single page of a book.

I was intrigued. Upon returning to my office, I asked our senior data analyst to pull from the database in which we keep our pricing information every instance where a price per hour was provided with a price per unit (sheet, page, scan, etc.). I selected one particular operation as a target sample. She checked and indeed, we could pull this pair-relationship out of the extensive data that we have. Not only that, but the data pair could be used to provide new information—how long it takes to do specific tasks.

All of the pair relationships for a single task were pulled out of the database and transferred into a spreadsheet where additional analysis was performed. She programmed the spreadsheet to generate the average time for each operation. She also commanded the software to calculate the amount of correlation between data samples.

Next, the timing results were compared with industry production standards from NAQP and NASS. She found a high correlation between our data and those of these two organizations. It's important to note, however, that our database partitions desktop services into finer detail (more tasks and functions).

This initiated a six month project to collect and tabulate timing information for every aspect of desktop design and layout including preflight operations such as data conversion, copy writing, keyboarding, and typography.

With over 26,000 companies in our database, identified only by state and ZIP code or Postal Mail Code (Canada), our sample size was large. Although the businesses in our database vary from one-person DTP shops operating out of a condo, to large prepress and printing firms with hundreds of employees, our results reflect the typical person on a typical machine. We were able to break out the time data by computer system, but with so many configurations available, this became unwieldy at best. Thus we decided to stick with the average time for the average employee working on a typical computer system.

The intent for our research, and this special report, is to help desktop service providers understand the typical times involved in performing specific tasks.

II. Machine Standards

"In business, competitors will always bite at your heels if you keep in the race, but if you stop running, they'll eat you alive."

Developing the Model

Machine standards are generated by listing the capabilities of your equipment and monitoring how long it takes a desktop system to perform a specific task. Input or output speed depends on the configuration of your system—the type of computer and peripheral devices, the organization of hard disk resources (fragmented files take longer to access) and the clock speed of each system. Computers can be purchased with clock speeds over 100 MHz, but the key factor is how long it takes that computer to perform a function. Although the CPU may be zipping along, the interface cards and the data bus on the system board may be limited to only 25 MHz. The slowest device determines the best speed possible in your electronic factory.

Besides the computer and hardware configuration, you'll also need to know the software used (including the version). By upgrading to a newer version of OCR software, we've been able to scan text two times faster than with the earlier software.

Include the set-up time to get ready to perform a task. Then specify the parameters of the input and output (e.g., image size, time to get the first output, and time to get subsequent outputs).

Typical Machine Standards

The following are typical machine standards for various desktop services. These time values are based on survey data and extensive research on-line and in trade literature and articles.

<table>
<tr><td>KEY:</td><td>cps = characters per second
mpp = minutes per page
ppm = pages per minute
sec/scn = seconds per scan
in/min = inches per minute
intp = interpolated</td></tr>
</table>

Scanner:

Scanner speed is determined by several factors: the scanner drive motor, how many passes it takes to complete a scan (single pass for B/W and some color scanners, or three passes for other color scanners), the amount of RAM in your computer (32 MB is probably the minimum for high resolution scans; 128 MB for large images), how the computer is connected to the scanner (serial or SCSI parallel), and how the scanner driver software manages memory. The ScanView DotMate 5000 can capture an RGB image with 36 bits per pixel at 1 MB per second. A Niscan Spectra can transfer 78 Kbps over its serial cable interface.

A high-end scanner can produce 15 to 20 scans an hour. A desktop drum scanner can produce 5 to 10 high res scans per hour. Drum scanners rotate at high speed (about 1600 rpm) and read a single line of pixels each revolution. By using multiple photomultiplier tubes (PMTs), a drum scanner can complete imaging in a single pass. Time depends on rotation speed, required resolution, size of original and final output, the computer system and the scanner output frequency. To scan an image at 5000 dpi with a drum rotating at 1600 rpm (26.67 revolutions per second), it takes 0.0375 seconds for each revolution. At 5000 pixels per inch, it takes 187.5 seconds to scan each inch of the image. Reduce the resolution required to 500 dpi and the time becomes only 18.75 seconds per inch. Thus the values in the tables below relate time to dpi.

Flatbed Scanners

Type	Rated Speed	
	(seconds per scan)	(comments)
Agfa DuoScan	35	4x5 @ 1000 dpi
Agfa Horizon Ultra	103	0.8ms/line @1200x2000dpi
Barneyscan CIS.3515	110	35mm slide @ 1000 dpi
DEST PC Scan 1000 series	20	page @ 300 dpi
HP Scanmaster	15	8.5 x 11 page @ 75 dpi
	50	8.5 x 11 page @ 300 dpi
HP Scanmaster ScanJet	20.4	@ 300 dpi,
	15	8.5 x 11 page @ 75 dpi
	59.8	same page @ 300 dpi
HP ScanJet IIc	28	4 x 5 color print @ 200 dpi
HP ScanJet 3c	30 - 80	full page @ 600 dpi
HP ScanJet 4p	7.5	monochrome @ 300 dpi
	30	full color @ 300 dpi
Howtek Scanmaster II	255	8 x 10 image
Lacie Silverscanner III	16	full page color scan preview
	59.7	final scan @ 4800 dpi intp
Microtek MSF 300 series	180	8.5x11 page @ 300 dpi
	9.9 - 11	same page @ 75 dpi
Microtek ScanMaker E6	38	5 x 7 color @ 300 dpi
Nikon LS-3510AF	90	35mm slide @ 1000 dpi
	89	test scan 2x2 final size
	74	final scan
Polaroid SprintScan 45	280	4x5 @ 2000 dpi
Prime Option Phovos 400C	50	color page @ 400 dpi
Screen FT-S700	80	5 x 5 original @ 4000 dpi
Sharp JX-300	255	8 x 10 image
Sharp JX-330	13	full page @ 300 dpi
Sharp JX-450	235	8 x 10 image

Type	Rated Speed	
	(seconds per scan)	(comments)
Umax Vista-S6	9	B/W scan @ 200 dpi
Umax Vista-S8 Color	7	B/W & GS @ 400x800 dpi
	15	4x5 color print @ 200 dpi
Xerox 730	14	page @ 300 dpi
	9	page @ 240,200,150 dpi
Visioneer PaperMax	60	8.5 x 11 page at 200 dpi
Epson ES-800C	90	A4-size page @ 400 dpi
Ricoh FS1S Color Scanner	50	A4-size page @ 400 dpi

Drum Scanners

Type	Rated Speed	
	(minutes/scan inch)	(comments)
DuPont Magnascan Plus	1.22	@ 1270 dpi
DuPont Crosfield C6000	5.76	@ 8000 dpi
Howtek ScanMaster 7500 Pro	3.13	@ 5000 dpi
Howtek ScanMaster 4500	3.33	@ 4000 dpi
Itek ICG 350iVertical	2.67	@ 4000 dpi
Linotype-Hell ChromaGraph S 3300	7.41	@ 10000 dpi
Optronics ColorGetter II Pro	5.75	5 x 7 transparency enlarged to 11 x 15 at 150 line screen)
Optronics ColorGetter 3 series	13.55	@ 8128 dpi
ScanView ScanMate Magic	2.0	@ 2000 dpi
ScanView ScanMate Plus II	2.17	@ 2600 dpi
ScanView ScanMate 4000	2.5	@ 4000 dpi
ScanView ScanMate 5000	3.13-5.0	@ 5000 dpi,
	1.0	@ 1600 dpi
Screen DT-S1051AI	2.08	@ 2500 dpi
Screen DT-S1030AI	4.33	@ 5200 dpi
Screen DT-S1045AI	6.67	@ 8000 dpi

Slide Scanner

Again lots of RAM in your computer improves machine speed. As much as 128 MB of RAM can dramatically reduce scan time for large images. Nikon suggests a minimum of 32 MB to achieve fast scans.

Type	Rated Speed	
	(minutes per scan)	(comments)
Barneyscan CIS.3515	1.83	35mm slide @ 1000 dpi
Barneyscan CIS.4520RS	9.0	35mm slide @ 2000 dpi
Howtek Scanmaster 35	3.3	@ 400 x 600 dpi color
	7.4	@ 1333 x 2000 dpi color
	16.67	@ 2000 x 3000 dpi color
	0.5	@ 400 x 600 dpi monochrome
	1.1	@ 1333x2000 dpi mono
	2.5	@ 2000x3000 dpi mono
Leafscan 35	3	35mm slide @ 4000 dpi
Leafscan LS-3510AF	1.83	full page 133 line screen @ 2048 x 1365 [8.3 MB]
Leafscan 45	4	35mm slide @ 5080 dpi
Microtek Scanmaker 1850S	3 - 4	35mm slide @ 1850 dpi
Minolta Quick Scan 35	0.2	12sec/slide @ 1000 dpi
Nikon LS-3510AF	1.5	35mm slide @ 3175 dpi
Nikon LS-3510AF	5.0	scanning a slide for printing on 8.5 x 11 paper @ 133 lpi yields image file size of about 8 MB (maximum scan rate 25-30 slides per hour)
	1.83	full page 133 line screen @ 2048 x 1365 pixels (8.3 MB)
Nikon Super CoolScan	0.67	40sec/slide @ 2700 dpi
Polaroid SprintScan 35	0.92	35mm slide @ 2700 dpi (one catalog ad stated 30 seconds for 2700 dpi, 30-bit slide scan)
ScanView ScanMate F8	2.22	27 scans/hr @ 4000 dpi

High Speed Scanner

Type	Rated Speed (images/minute)	(comments)
BancTec TDC DS-2610W	96	@ 300 dpi 2 min 3 sec for 250 checks, 2 min 9 sec for 250 sheets of 8.5 x 11 bond paper, 2 minutes 3 sec for 250 pages 8.5 x 11 magazine pages)
BancTec DocuScan 4000 series	100+	@ 300 dpi
Bell & Howell CopiScan II 2	137	48 ppm @ 200 dpi
Bell & Howell Copiscan II 2	138	72 @ 200 dpi (43.3 seconds for 20 FedEx forms) (2 minutes 38 sec for 250 checks) (2 minutes 49 seconds for 250 pages of 8.5 x 11 bond paper) (2 minutes 51 sec for 250 8.5 x 11 magazine pages
Bell & Howell Copiscan II 3338	42 ppm	@ 300 dpi
Bell & Howell Copiscan II 6338	84	@ 300 dpi
Cognitronics CIP/200	100 ppm	@ 120 dpi
	30 ppm	@ 200 dpi
Fujitsu M3093E	25 ppm	@ 400 dpi
Fujitsu M3096E+	20 ppm	@ 400 dpi
Fujitsu M3097E	39 ppm	@ 400 dpi
Fujitsu M3099A	100	@ 400 dpi
Fujitsu M3097E/G	39	@ 300 dpi
Ideal IDVS-1117	36	@ 200 dpi
	19 ppm	@ 400 dpi
Kodak Imagelink 923 S/D	144	@ 200 dpi
	48 ppm	@ 300 dpi
Kodak Imagelink 500 S/D	60	@ 300 dpi
Microseal VS-1255	36	@ 200 dpi
	18 ppm	@ 400 dpi

Type	Rated Speed (images/minute)	(comments)
Panasonic IS-331	20	@ 400 dpi
Panasonic KV-SP500/505	40	@ 300 dpi
Photomatrix 6000 series	183	@ 300 dpi
Photomatrix 4000 series	60	@ 200 dpi
Ricoh IS410	20	@ 400 dpi
Ricoh IS510	48	@ 400 dpi
Ricoh IS520	48	@ 400 dpi simplex
	96	@ 400 dpi duplex
	10 in/sec	@ 200 dpi
Southern Comp Sys ImageTrac	90	@ 200 dpi
TDC DocuScan 4000 series	48	@ 300 dpi duplex
TDC DocuScan 2000 series	54	@ 200 dpi,
	43 ppm	@ 300 dpi
Visionshape VS-1000	36	@ 400 dpi
Visionshape VS-1250	40	@ 400 dpi
Visionshape VS-1251	40	@ 400 dpi
Visionshape VS-2500	40	@ 400 dpi

Large Format Scanner

Type	Rated Speed (inch/sec, sec/image)	(comments)
Houston Instrument LDS 4000+	2 to 8 inch/sec	@ 200 dpi
Scangraphics CF 400/36	30 sec/image	@ 200 dpi (E-size image)

Microform Scanner

Type	Rated Speed (images/minute)	(comments)
Mekel M400XL Roll Film Scanner	85	
Mekel M460XL Microfiche Scanner	85	

Film Recorder

Here speed is directly related to the conversion time to translate a digital file into digital dots (rasterization) and to then convert the rasterized image into video signals to drive a film recorder (recording cycle or light-on-film cycle). Rasterization often takes longer than recording. A common rating is to record at 4 KB resolution in about 100 seconds.

The problem with digital film recorders is that exposing the digital images to film is more time consuming than analog film recorders— as long as five to 15 minutes. The film recorder is integrated with the hardware and software connected to it. The software must translate the data into the film recorder's format. Complex slides (not image files) take longer to expose than simple slides. Complex image files can lock up a film recorder. In addition the film recorder's driver software can be poorly written causing slides to require even more processing time.

The real issue isn't so much speed as it is system throughput. It can take between one and four hours to expose the film. In addition, two film recorders might expend significantly different time to complete a 30-slide presentation. A $100,000 film recorder could image in 90 seconds, while a $10,000 recorder could take 15 minutes (900 seconds).

There is a minor quality difference between 2K and 4K slides, but most users prefer 4K imaging. Imaging 20 to 30 slides at 4K takes about 40 minutes more than imaging at 2K.

Most slides shoot in about a minute with a black background. If a bright color is behind the graphics, the imaging time can push out to six minutes or more. As you push toward higher resolution, say 8K, an image of 8,192 x 5,461 pixels requires 45 million pixels for each color (135 million pixels total). This increases the record and processing time.

To compare apples with apples, I've listed the 35mm imaging speed for various film recorders at a resolution of 4K and typical complexity. The timing values are based on manufacturer's specifications.

Type	Rated Speed (minutes/4K slide)	(comments)
2Film Technologies F2FR	1.0	2K slide
Agfa		
Alto	0.5	
Alto LE	0.5	
PCR II	0.5 to 1.05	
ProColor Premier	1.05	
Bell & Howell		
Color Dig Imager IV	0.47	
Celco		
8000A	0.33	
800B	0.33	
5000A	0.33	
5000B	0.33	
Junior	1.0	
Micro	1.0	
Cymbolic Sciences		
LightJet 2040	5.0	8x10 @ 1016 lpi (RES 40)
LightJet 2080	10	8x10 at 2,032 lpi (RES 80)
Focus Graphics ImageCorder	0.33	2K slide
	0.25	full color image
GCC Technologies ColorFast II	1.5	
General Parametrics		
PhotoMetric	1 to 6	
SpectraStar O50	1.83	
Genigraphics		
8770	0.5	
8780	0.5	
Graf Tel Sys Model Viewer DC100	1 to 5	
Lasergraphics		
LFR	2	
	1.2 to 2.04	2K slide
LFR Mark II	0.75 to 2.0	
LFR Mark III	0.67 to 4.83	8K
LFR-X	0.67 to 1.5	
Personal LFR	1.5	

Type	Rated Speed minutes/4K slide	comments
Management Graphics		
Sapphire	0.5 to 0.83	
Solitare IFR	1.33	
Solitare	0.72 to 2.67	
Solitare 16xps	0.5	
Matrix Instruments		
PCR	0.5	
ProColor	0.5	
SlideWriter	0.5	
QCR-Z	1	
Mirus		
Galleria	5 to 6	
Turbo II	1.5 to 3	
Turbo PC	1.5 to 3	
Polaroid		
Digital Palette CI-3000S	0.75 to 2	2K slide
Digital Palette CI-5000S	1.5 to 3	
Palette Plus	0.75 to 2	
Turbo Palette	0.75 to 2	
Bravo Computer Slide Mkr	6 to 12	
Presentation Technologies		
ImageMaker	8 to 10	
Montage FR1	3 to 6	
Montage FR2	1.83 to 3	
	3.38	2K slide
Prime Option		
Still Light 3.0	3.0	
Verite II	1.5	

OCR Scanner

Type	Rated Speed (words/minute)
Umax ReadStation	1,500 wpm

Photo CD Mastering

Type	Rated Speed (minutes/disc)
Print Photo CD Workstation	39 minutes/650 MB disc

Outputting CD ROM files

Type	Rated Speed (sec/file)	(comments)
Apple CD 300	12	small files
	52	database files
	68	large files
	62	multisession Photo CD
OAI CD/Turbo 6-Pak	12	small files
	50	database files
	75	large files
	69	multisession Photo CD
Toshiba TXM3401E1	12	small files
	60	database files
	73	large files
	62	multisession Photo CD

Type	Rated Speed	
	sec/file	comments
Texel DM-5024	14	small files
	64	database files
	80	large files
	77	multisession Photo CD
NEC MultiSpin 74	17	small files
	68	database files
	76	large files
	88	multisession Photo CD

Inkjet Printer

Inkjet Printer	Rated Speed (pages/minute - ppm) (characters/second - cps)
Apple	
StyleWriter 1200	3.0 ppm
Color StyleWriter 1500	0.3 ppm (color), 3.0 ppm (black)
Color StyleWriter 2200	0.33 ppm (color), 5.0 ppm (black)
Color StyleWriter 2400	0.3 ppm (color), 3.0 ppm (black)
Color StyleWriter 2500	0.66 ppm (color), 5.0 ppm (black)
Brother	
HJ400	110 cps
CalComp	
TechJet Personal	248 cps
Canon	
BJ-10sx	1.8-3.0 ppm / 110 cps
BJ-200e	173- 248 cps
BJ-200 ex	4.1 ppm (204-248 cps)
BJC-210	0.27 ppm (color), 4 ppm (black)
BJ-230	4 ppm (248 cps)
BJC-30	277 cps
BJC-4000	0.8-8.2 ppm (346-496 cps)
BJC-4100	0.8 ppm (2-6 ppm mono)

Inkjet Printer	Rated Speed (pages/minute - ppm) (characters/second - cps)
Canon (contd.)	
BJC-600/600e	170-240 cps (1 ppm color)
BJC-610	0.7 ppm (1ppm graphics, 3 ppm text)
BJC-800	2.0 ppm
BJC-820	300 cps
Digital Equipment Corp.	
DECWriter 90	2.0 ppm
DECWriter 100I	3.0 ppm
DECWriter 110I	2.2 ppm
DECWriter 500I	5.0 ppm
Epson	
Stylus 800+	2.7 ppm
Stylus 1000	2.5 ppm
Stylus Color II	1.0 ppm
Stylus Photo 700 color	8x10 photo < 5 min @1440x720 dpi
Stylus Pro	2.0 ppm
Hewlett Packard	
DeskJet 560C	3.0 ppm (1.5 minutes/page - color)
DeskJet 600C	4 ppm
DeskJet 660C	1.5 ppm(color), 4 ppm (black)
DeskJet 680C	1.5 ppm (color), 5 ppm (black)
DeskJet 820Cxi	4 ppm (color), 6.5 ppm (black)
DeskJet 850C	2.0 ppm
DeskJet 855Cxi	3 ppm (color), 7 ppm (black)
DeskJet 1200C/PS	7.0 ppm (2 minutes/page - color) 9 ppm (black, text)
Deskjet Portable	3.0 ppm
DeskWriter 540	1.3-3.0 ppm
DeskWriter 560C	3.0 ppm (1.5 minutes/page)
DeskWriter 660C	1.5 ppm
Lexmark	
ExecJet 4072 Color	150-300 cps
ExecJet II 4076	3.0 ppm
ExecJet IIc	120-240 cps (color) / 0.2 ppm 167-300 cps (black)

Inkjet Printer	Rated Speed (pages/minute - ppm) (characters/second - cps)
Lexmark (contd.)	
ExecJet iic 407602c	0.14 ppm
Jetprinter 2070	1.0 ppm
Color Jetprinter PS 4079	0.7 ppm
Mannesmann Tally	
MobileJet	100 cps
Okidata	
OkiJet 2010	3.0 ppm
Pacific Data Products	
ProTracer II	300 cps
TI	
MicroMarc	4.0 ppm
MicroMarc Color	1.0 ppm
Xerox	
XJ3	3.0 ppm
XJ5	5.0 ppm

Thermal Printer

Thermal Printer	Rated Speed (pages/minute - ppm) (minutes/page - mpp)
Citizen	
Notebook Printer II	2 ppm
PN60 Portable	2 ppm
Hewlett Packard	
DeskJet 320 Thermal	2 ppm (color), 3 ppm (black)
DeskJet 540 Thermal	2 ppm (color)
	3 ppm (black)
	1 ppm (black, presentation)
	1.5-2.5 mpp (color)
	4.0 mpp (color, draft quality)
DeskWriter 540 Thermal	1.0-3.0 ppm (black)
	1.5-4.0 mpp (color)
DeskWriter 660C Thermal	1.5 ppm (color), 4 ppm (black)

Thermal Printer	Rated Speed (pages/minute - ppm) (minutes/page - mpp)	
Howtek		
Pixelmaster	2-3 mpp	
Kodak		
ColorEase PS (color)	3.5 mpp	
XLS 8600 (color)	1 ppm / 1.2 mpp	
XLS 8600 PS (color)	1 ppm / 1.2 mpp	
XLT 7720 (color)	1.6-3.2 mpp	
Fargo		
Primera (color)	0.4 ppm	
PrimeraPro (color)	0.75 ppm	(dye sub)
General Parametrics		
SpectraStar Gtx	2 ppm	(color)
SpectraStar Dtx	1.75 mpp (color)	
Genicom		
7025	2.5 mpp (color)	
Lexmark		
ColorJet 4079 plus	1.0 ppm (color), 1.7 ppm (black)	
WinWriter 150C	167-300 cps	
Mannesmann		
MobileWriter	6 ppm	
NEC		
SuperScript Color 3000	1-10 ppm	(color)
QMS		
ColorScript 210	1 ppm	(color)
ColorScript 230	1 ppm	(color)
Radius		
Proof Positive 3.0 (full-page)		6 mpp (color)
Proof Positive 3.0 (two-page)		12 mpp (color)
Seiko		
Personal ColorPoint PSE	0.5	(color)
Siemens		
2030	30	
2040	40	
Star		
SJ-144		306 cps (color)
Tektronix Phaser 240	2 ppm	600x300 (color)

LED Printer

LED Printer	Rated Speed (pages/minute - ppm) (characters/second - cps)
Kyocera	
FS1600A	10 ppm
FS3600	18 ppm
Lexmark	
ValueWriter 300	5 ppm
ValueWriter 600	5 ppm
Okidata	
OL400e	4 ppm
OL410e / OL410ePS	4 ppm
OL810e	8 ppm
OL1200	12 ppm

Laser Printer (≥ 600 dpi)

Laser Printer	Rated Speed (pages / minute) (comments)
Advanced Technologies	
LC-6820	20 ppm
LC-6822	20 ppm
LC-6832	32 ppm
Analog Technology	
8030	16 ppm
Apple	
LaserWriter 4/600 PS	4 ppm
LaserWriter 16/600 PS	17 ppm
LaserWriter Select 360	10 ppm
Personal LaserWriter 320	4 ppm
Brother	
HI-10V, h	10 ppm
HL-630	6 ppm
HL-645	6 ppm
HL-655M	6 ppm
HL-660	6 ppm

Laser Printer	**Rated Speed**	
	(pages / minute)	(comments)
Brother (contd.)		
HL-960	12 ppm	
HL-1260	12 ppm	
HL-1660	16 ppm	
WL-660	6 ppm	
CalComp		
CCL 1200ES	16 ppm	
CCL 600	8 ppm	
CCL 600ES	16 ppm	
Canon		
LBP-430	4 ppm	
LBP-4sx	4 ppm	
LBP-860	8 ppm	
Citizen		
ProLaser 6000	6 ppm	
DataProducts		
Typhoon 20	20 ppm	
Typhoon 30	30 ppm	
Digital Equipment Corp.		
DECLaser 1152	4 ppm	
DECLaser 3500	12 ppm	
DECLaser 5100	8 ppm	
Epson		
ActionLaser 1100	4 ppm	
ActionLaser 1400	4 ppm	
ActionLaser 1500	6 ppm	
ActionLaser 1600	6 ppm	
Fujitsu		
Print Partner 30	30 ppm	
Print Partner 30I	30 ppm	
Print Partner 4000	4 ppm	
Print Partner 8000	8 ppm	
GCC		
Elite 600et	10 ppm	
Genicom		
7610	10 ppm	
7612	12 ppm	

Laser Printer	Rated Speed (pages / minute)	(comments)
Genicom (contd.)		
9160	16 ppm	
9170	17 ppm	
Hewlett Packard		
Color LaserJet	1 ppm	(4 color,- transparency)
	2 ppm	(4 color, document)
	10 ppm	(black, document)
LaserJet 4 Plus	12 ppm	
LaserJet 4M	8 ppm	
LaserJet 4M Plus	12 ppm	
LaserJet 4MP	4 ppm	
LaserJet 4MV	16 ppm	
LaserJet 4P	4 ppm	
LaserJet 4Si	17 ppm	
LaserJet 4Si MX	17 ppm	
LaserJet 4V	16 ppm	
LaserJet 5L-FS	4 ppm	
LaserJet 5P	6 ppm	
LaserJet 5MP	6 ppm	
IBM		
4039 series	8 ppm	
IDEA 13x38	16 ppm	
Konica		
LP3110	10 ppm	
LP3210	10 ppm	
Kyocera		
FS-1500A	10 ppm	
FS-1600A	10 ppm	
FS-3600A	18 ppm	
LaserMaster		
WinPrinter 600XL	8 ppm	
WinPrinter 800	4 ppm	
WinPrinter 1000	4 ppm	
Unity 1800PM-R	10 ppm	
Unity 1800 XL	8 ppm	
Unity 1800XL-O	8 ppm	

Laser Printer	Rated Speed (pages / minute)	(comments)
Lexmark		
4039-10 Plus	10 ppm	
4039-10R	8 ppm	
4039-12L	12 ppm	
LaserPrinter 10plus	10 ppm	
Optra C	3 ppm	color
Optra E	6 ppm	
Optra Lx / Rx	8 ppm	@ 1200 dpi
	16 ppm	@ 600 dpi
Optra Lx+	8 ppm	
Optra Lxi	16 ppm	
Optra Lxi+	8 ppm	
Optra N	24 ppm	
Optra R	12 ppm	
Optra R+/Rt+	8 ppm	
ValueWriter 600	5 ppm	
WinWriter 150c	3 ppm	
WinWriter 600	8 ppm	@ 600 dpi
	10 ppm	@ 300 dpi
Mannesmann		
T9008	8 ppm	
Minolta		
PageWorks 20	20 ppm	@ 600 dpi
NEC		
SilentWriter SuperScript 610	6 ppm	
SilentWriter SuperScript 660	6 ppm	660i does 8 ppm
SuperScript 1260	12 ppm	@600 dpi
NewGen		
DesignXpress series	16 ppm	(letter)
	9 ppm	(ledger)
DesignXpress 6	16 ppm	
ImagerPlus 6L	8 ppm	
Turbo PS/660	6 ppm	
Okidata		
OL600e/610e	6 ppm	
OL810e/830	8 ppm	
Okipage 16n	16 ppm	@1200x600 dpi

Laser Printer	Rated Speed (pages / minute)	(comments)
QMS		
1060 Print System	10 ppm	
1660 Print System	16 ppm	
1725 SLS	17 ppm	
2001 Knowledge System	6 ppm	
3825 Print System	38 ppm	
Magicolor laser	2 -8 ppm	
Panasonic		
KX-P6500	6ppm	@600 dpi
Samsung		
Finale 8000	8 ppm	
Sharp		
JX-9460PS	6 ppm	
JX-9660PS	8 ppm	
Star Micronics		
LS-5EX	5 ppm	
TI		
microLaser 600	5 ppm	
microLaser PowerPro	12 ppm	
microLaser Pro E	12 ppm	
microLaser Pro 600 PS23	8 ppm	
microLaser WIN/4	4 ppm	
Xante		
Accel-a-Writer 8200	16 ppm	
LaserPress 1200	8 ppm	
Xerox		
4505	5 ppm	
4510ps	10 ppm	
4520mp	20 ppm	
8808	8 ppm	

Large Format Printers

Printer	Rated Speed (comments)
Canon	
2436 Color Bubble-Jet Copier	6 min. (24"x36" image @ 400 dpi)
ColorSpan	
DesignWinder Professional	25 min (36" E poster @600 dpi)
Computer Image Systems	
Custom airbrush printer	90 min. (14' x 18' billboard)
Data Technologies	
CJ300 Flatbed Inkjet Plotter	45 min. (6' x 4' image @ 300 dpi)
	15-20 min. (6' x 4' image, draft)
EnCAD	
NovaJet III	15 min. (4C, 24" x 36" @ 600 dpi)
	45 min (36x48 poster @ 300 dpi)
NovaJet Pro	13 min. (4C, 24" x 36" @ 300 dpi)
NovaJet Pro 6002	29 sq ft/hr @ 600 dpi
LaserMaster	
DisplayMaker	50 minutes (34" x 44" image)
DisplayMaker Express	330 sq in/min (54" wide)
	5 minutes (34" x 44" image)
Metromedia Technologies	
Custom acrylic paint spray	2 hours (14' x 48' image)
Océ-Bruning	
Océ 9800	8 E-size pages/minute @ 400 dpi
	14.5 D-size pages/min. @ 400 dpi
Pixmil	
Custom acrylic paint spray	1 hour (1' x 62' strip)
	16 hours (16' x 62' image @ 7.5-30 pixels/inch)
Raster Graphics	
DCS 5400	500 sq ft/hr (52" wide, 200 dpi)
	(10 minutes to do eight 36" x 48" posters)
Scitex	
Outboard color inkjet	540 sq ft/hr (63" wide, 10-20 dpi)
Xerox	
Colorgrafx 8954 plotter	3 minutes (54" wide, 200-400 dpi)

High Speed Network Printer

NetworkPrinter	Rated Speed (pages/minute - ppm)
NewGen	
DesignXpress 6	16 ppm
Compaq	
PageMarq 20	20 ppm
Datco/Derex	
S3030 LED	30 ppm
Digital Electric Corp.	
DEC PrintServer 32	32 ppm
Lexmark	
Optra N	24 ppm
Olympus	
MegaServe	30 / 45 ppm
Printronix	
L2324-NET	24 ppm
QMS	
PS 3200	32 ppm
Sharp	
AO-4100P	40 ppm ltr size 20 ppm legal size
Talaris	
5093	50 ppm
Xerox	
DocuPrint 390	92 ppm
DocuPrint 4232	30 ppm @ 600 dpi

Imagesetter

Imagesetter	Rated Speed (inches/ minute)	(comments)
Agfa		
AccuSet	7	@ 3000 dpi
SelectSet 5000	11.7	@ 3500 dpi
SelectSet 7000	12.7	@ 3600 dpi
ProSet 9550	9.7	@ 2400 dpi

Imagesetter	Rated Speed (inches/ minute)	(comments)
Autologic		
APS-Colormaster	4.7	@ 2540 dpi
APS Platemaster		79 seconds
		(20 x 26 inch page @1016 dpi)
APS-6/108C	14.1	@ 1446 dpi
APS-5000/7000		3 minutes
		(22 x 15.7 inch page @3600 dpi)
APS-6/82 ACS	6	@ 3000 dpi
APS-6/108	47.2	@ 1016 dpi
ECRM		
ScriptSetter I	4.13	@ 2540 dpi
ScriptSetter III	4	@ 2540 dpi
ScriptSetter IV	4.13	@ 2540 dpi
Escher Grad		
EG-8000	0.03	@ 6000 dpi
Hyphen		
Spectraset 2400	5	@ 3000 dpi
Spectraset 3200	4	@ 3600 dpi
Spectraset 3000	2.4	@ 3000 dpi
Dash 72E/94E	3.5	@ 3000 dpi
Dash 72P/94P	1.7	@ 3000 dpi
Imapro		
Output Station	4	
Intergraph ColorSetter 4000		20 Mpixels/sec
Linotronic-Hell		
L-70	4.5	@ 1200 dpi
L-90	4.5	@ 1200 dpi
L-260 RIP 40	3.9	@ 2540 dpi
	4.9	@ 2032 dpi
	8.7	@ 1693 dpi
	15.8	@ 1270 dpi
	23.0	@ 845 dpi
	31	@ 635 dpi
L-330 RIP 50	3.8	@ 3386 dpi
L-530 RIP 50	5.3	@ 2540 dpi
L-630 RIP 60	4.4	@ 3251 dpi
L-830 RIP 50	3.8	@ 3251 dpi
L-930 RIP 50	3.8	@ 3251 dpi

Imagesetter	Rated Speed (inches/ minute)	(comments)
Monotype		
ExpressMaster 1000	30	@ 1000 dpi
ExpressMaster 1016	24	@ 1016 dpi
ExpressMaster 1200	25	@ 1200 dpi
ExpressMaster 1270	19	@ 1270 dpi
ExpressMaster 2000	4.1	@ 2540 dpi
ExpressMaster 3850	13	@ 1600 dpi
ImageMaster 1000	6	@ 3000 dpi
ImageMaster 2000	4	@ 2540 dpi
ImageMaster 3000	3.3	@ 3048 dpi
ImageMaster 5000	4	@ 3600 dpi
ImageMaster 7000	4	@ 3600 dpi
Optronics		
ColorSetter 2000II	260 sq in/min	@ 2000 dpi
ColorSetter XL 2000	235 sq in/min	
ColorSetter 4000	65 sq in/min	@ 4000 dpi
ColorSetter XL 4000	63 sq in/min	
DeskSetter 3000	30 sq in/min	
Printware		
3240 Film Imager	18	@ 1800 dpi
1440 EZ Platesetter	40	@ 1200 dpi
Purup		
Prepress ImageMaker 80/10	4.7	
Scitex America		
Dolev 800	831 sq in/min @ 1270 dpi	
Screen		
DT-R103S	0.6	
MT-R1100	0.6	
FT-R1050	6	
Strobbe		
Laser Composer	6.6	
Varityper		
VT600P	10 ppm (letter)	@ 600 dpi
	8 ppm (legal)	@ 600 dpi
Varityper Series 6000	7.9	@ 3048 dpi

Other Devices

Canon Color Copier/Printer
    CLC 1000   31 ppm (first copy in 15 sec)
Ricoh Color Copier/Printer
    Aficio 5000   31 ppm BW, 6 ppm color
Polaroid Color Proofing System
    DryJet II w/RIP   12 A3 page/hr @ 600 dpi
Kodak Digital Camera
    DCS 460 w/Canon EOS-1N   2 images in 2 seconds burst rate
                                           8 sec pause for storing image

Leaf Digital Camera Back
    DCB II   captures live video at 4 frames/sec

Forms for Developing Machine Standards

Next are sample forms to help you develop your own machine standards. Each process includes an example and blank worksheets that you can use to generate custom machine standards. Similar worksheet templates are contained in the software that came with this special report.

After enough data samples have been collected, averaging the set-up time, and the process time will produce machine standards for each function—standards that you can use in calculating your own budgeted hourly rates.

SECONDS TO MINUTES CONVERSION TABLE

10 seconds = 0.17 minutes	35 seconds = 0.58 minutes
15 seconds = 0.25 minutes	40 seconds = 0.67 minutes
20 seconds = 0.33 minutes	45 seconds = 0.75 minutes
25 seconds = 0.42 minutes	50 seconds = 0.83 minutes
30 seconds = 0.50 minutes	55 seconds = 0.92 minutes

Example - Scanning
Machine Standards

B/W Line Art

Effective Date: *January 30, 1999*

Hardware: *486DX, 100 MHz, 16 MB RAM, 520 MB HD, SCSI interface, Scanmaster, 50 sec/pg, 300 dpi*

Software: *Ofoto v 1.5*

Start-Up / Set-Up Time (minutes)	Original Image Size (sq inches)	Resolution (dpi)	Scan Rate (minutes/inch)
3.3	12	300	4.1
3.1	11	300	4.0
3.4	16.5	300	3.9

Average Start-up Set-up Time (minutes)	Average Image Size (sq in)	Average Scan Resolution (dpi)	Average Scan Rate (minutes/inch)
2.17	13.2	300	4.0

Scanning
Machine Standards
B/W Line Art

Effective Date: ________________________

Hardware: ____

____

Software: ____

Start-Up / Set-Up Time (minutes)	Original Image Size (sq inches)	Resolution (dpi)	Scan Rate (minutes/inch)
__________	__________	__________	__________
__________	__________	__________	__________
__________	__________	__________	__________
__________	__________	__________	__________
__________	__________	__________	__________
__________	__________	__________	__________
__________	__________	__________	__________
__________	__________	__________	__________
__________	__________	__________	__________
__________	__________	__________	__________
__________	__________	__________	__________
__________	__________	__________	__________
__________	__________	__________	__________
__________	__________	__________	__________
__________	__________	__________	__________
__________	__________	__________	__________
__________	__________	__________	__________

Average Start-up Set-up Time (minutes)	Average Image Size (sq in)	Average Scan Resolution (dpi)	Average Scan Rate (minutes/inch)

Scanning
Machine Standards
Gray Scale

Effective Date: _______________________

Hardware: ____

____

Software: ____

Start-Up / Set-Up Time (minutes)	Original Image Size (sq inches)	Resolution (dpi)	Scan Rate (minutes/inch)
_______________	_______________	_______________	_______________
_______________	_______________	_______________	_______________
_______________	_______________	_______________	_______________
_______________	_______________	_______________	_______________
_______________	_______________	_______________	_______________
_______________	_______________	_______________	_______________
_______________	_______________	_______________	_______________
_______________	_______________	_______________	_______________
_______________	_______________	_______________	_______________
_______________	_______________	_______________	_______________
_______________	_______________	_______________	_______________
_______________	_______________	_______________	_______________
_______________	_______________	_______________	_______________
_______________	_______________	_______________	_______________
_______________	_______________	_______________	_______________

Average Start-up Set-up Time (minutes)	Average Image Size (sq in)	Average Scan Resolution (dpi)	Average Scan Rate (minutes/inch)

Scanning
Machine Standards
B/W Photographs

Effective Date: _______________________

Hardware: ____

____

Software: ____

Start-Up / Set-Up Time (minutes)	Original Image Size (sq inches)	Resolution (dpi)	Scan Rate (minutes/inch)
_______	_______	_______	_______
_______	_______	_______	_______
_______	_______	_______	_______
_______	_______	_______	_______
_______	_______	_______	_______
_______	_______	_______	_______
_______	_______	_______	_______
_______	_______	_______	_______
_______	_______	_______	_______
_______	_______	_______	_______
_______	_______	_______	_______
_______	_______	_______	_______
_______	_______	_______	_______
_______	_______	_______	_______
_______	_______	_______	_______
_______	_______	_______	_______
_______	_______	_______	_______

Average Start-up Set-up Time (minutes)	Average Image Size (sq in)	Average Scan Resolution (dpi)	Average Scan Rate (minutes/inch)

Scanning
Machine Standards

Color Illustrations

Effective Date: _______________________

Hardware: ____

____

Software: ____

Start-Up / Set-Up Time (minutes)	Original Image Size (sq inches)	Resolution (dpi)	Scan Rate (minutes/inch)
__________	__________	__________	__________
__________	__________	__________	__________
__________	__________	__________	__________
__________	__________	__________	__________
__________	__________	__________	__________
__________	__________	__________	__________
__________	__________	__________	__________
__________	__________	__________	__________
__________	__________	__________	__________
__________	__________	__________	__________
__________	__________	__________	__________
__________	__________	__________	__________
__________	__________	__________	__________
__________	__________	__________	__________
__________	__________	__________	__________
__________	__________	__________	__________

Average Start-up Set-up Time (minutes)	Average Image Size (sq in)	Average Scan Resolution (dpi)	Average Scan Rate (minutes/inch)

Scanning
Machine Standards
Color Photographs

Effective Date: _______________________

Hardware: ____
____

Software: ____

Start-Up / Set-Up Time (minutes)	Original Image Size (sq inches)	Resolution (dpi)	Scan Rate (minutes/inch)
_______	_______	_______	_______
_______	_______	_______	_______
_______	_______	_______	_______
_______	_______	_______	_______
_______	_______	_______	_______
_______	_______	_______	_______
_______	_______	_______	_______
_______	_______	_______	_______
_______	_______	_______	_______
_______	_______	_______	_______
_______	_______	_______	_______
_______	_______	_______	_______
_______	_______	_______	_______
_______	_______	_______	_______
_______	_______	_______	_______
_______	_______	_______	_______
_______	_______	_______	_______

Average Start-up Set-up Time (minutes)	Average Image Size (sq in)	Average Scan Resolution (dpi)	Average Scan Rate (minutes/inch)

Scanning
Machine Standards
Optical Character Recognition

Effective Date: ___________________

Hardware: ____

____

Software: ____

Start-Up / Set-Up Time (minutes)	Original Image Size (sq inches)	Resolution (dpi)	Scan Rate (minutes/inch)	Scan Rate (minutes/inch)
______	______	______	______	______
______	______	______	______	______
______	______	______	______	______
______	______	______	______	______
______	______	______	______	______
______	______	______	______	______
______	______	______	______	______
______	______	______	______	______
______	______	______	______	______
______	______	______	______	______
______	______	______	______	______
______	______	______	______	______
______	______	______	______	______
______	______	______	______	______
______	______	______	______	______
______	______	______	______	______
______	______	______	______	______

Average Start-Up / Set-Up Time (minutes)	Average Image Size (sq inches)	Average Resolution (dpi)	Average Scan Rate (minutes/inch)	Average Scan Rate (minutes/inch)

EXAMPLE - Printer Output
Machine Standards

$$\text{B/W Plain Paper Laser Typesetting}$$

System Configuration: Effective Date: _January 15, 1999_
    Computer: _PowerMac, 100 MHz, 16 MB RAM, 520 MB HD_
    Laser Printer: _LaserWriter 16/600 PS, 17 ppm_
Print Resolution: _600 dpi_   File Type: _PM 5.1 w/imported PICT_
Start-up/Set-up Time: _4 minutes_   Sheet Size: _8.5 x 11_

Page #	Page Printing Time (seconds) text only	30% art	70% art	Page #	Page Printing Time (seconds) text only	30% art	70% art
1	13			16			
2		24		17			
3			35	18			
4	12			19			
5		31		20			
6			47	21			
7	13			22			
8				23			
9				24			
10				25			
11				26			
12				27			
13				28			
14				29			
15				30			

Total # Pages	text only	30% art	70% art	Total Print Time	text only	30% art	70% art
	3	2	2		38	55	82

Average Printing Time at	text only	30% art	70% art
	12.6	27.5	41.0

Printer Output
Machine Standards

B/W Plain Paper Laser Typesetting

System Configuration: Effective Date: _______________________

   Computer: ____

   Laser Printer: ____

Print Resolution: _________   File Type: __________________________

Start-up/Set-up Time: _________   Sheet Size: ___________________

Page #	Page Printing Time (seconds) text only	30% art	70% art
1			
2			
3			
4			
5			
6			
7			
8			
9			
10			
11			
12			
13			
14			
15			

Page #	Page Printing Time (seconds) text only	30% art	70% art
16			
17			
18			
19			
20			
21			
22			
23			
24			
25			
26			
27			
28			
29			
30			

Total # Pages	text only	30% art	70% art

Total Print Time	text only	30% art	70% art

Average Printing Time at	text only	30% art	70% art

Printer Output

Machine Standards

Color Laser Typesetting

System Configuration: Effective Date: _______________________

Computer:____

Laser Printer:____

Print Resolution:________   File Type:__________________________

Start-up/Set-up Time:________   Sheet Size: __________________

Page Printing Time (seconds)			
Page #	text only	30% art	70% art
1			
2			
3			
4			
5			
6			
7			
8			
9			
10			
11			
12			
13			
14			
15			

Page Printing Time (seconds)			
Page #	text only	30% art	70% art
16			
17			
18			
19			
20			
21			
22			
23			
24			
25			
26			
27			
28			
29			
30			

Total # Pages	text only	30% art	70% art

Total Print Time	text only	30% art	70% art

Average Printing Time at	text only	30% art	70% art

Printer Output
Machine Standards
Inkjet Printing

System Configuration: Effective Date: _______________________
    Computer: ____
    Laser Printer: ____
Print Resolution: _________   File Type: ______________________
Start-up/Set-up Time: _______   Sheet Size: ___________________

Page Printing Time (seconds)				Page Printing Time (seconds)			
Page #	text only	30% art	70% art	Page #	text only	30% art	70% art
1				16			
2				17			
3				18			
4				19			
5				20			
6				21			
7				22			
8				23			
9				24			
10				25			
11				26			
12				27			
13				28			
14				29			
15				30			

Total # Pages	text only	30% art	70% art	Total Print Time	text only	30% art	70% art

Average Printing Time at	text only	30% art	70% art

Printer Output
Machine Standards
Thermal Printing

System Configuration: Effective Date: ___________________
  Computer:____
  Laser Printer:_______________________________________
Print Resolution:________   File Type:_____________________
Start-up/Set-up Time:_______   Sheet Size: ________________

| Page Printing Time (seconds) | | | | Page Printing Time (seconds) | | | |
Page #	text only	30% art	70% art	Page #	text only	30% art	70% art
1				16			
2				17			
3				18			
4				19			
5				20			
6				21			
7				22			
8				23			
9				24			
10				25			
11				26			
12				27			
13				28			
14				29			
15				30			

Total # Pages	text only	30% art	70% art	Total Print Time	text only	30% art	70% art

Average Printing Time at	text only	30% art	70% art

Imagesetter Output
Machine Standards
RC Paper

System Configuration: Effective Date: _______________

  Computer:____

  Laser Printer:_____________________________________

Print Resolution:________   File Type:_________________

Start-up/Set-up Time:________   Sheet Size: _______________

Page #	Page Printing Time (seconds) text only	30% art	70% art
1			
2			
3			
4			
5			
6			
7			
8			
9			
10			
11			
12			
13			
14			
15			

Page #	Page Printing Time (seconds) text only	30% art	70% art
16			
17			
18			
19			
20			
21			
22			
23			
24			
25			
26			
27			
28			
29			
30			

Total # Pages	text only	30% art	70% art

Total Print Time	text only	30% art	70% art

Average Printing Time at	text only	30% art	70% art

Imagesetter Output

Machine Standards

Film

System Configuration: Effective Date: _______________________

  Computer: ____

  Laser Printer: ____

Print Resolution: __________   File Type: ___________________________

Start-up/Set-up Time: _________   Sheet Size: ____________________

	Page Printing Time (seconds)		
Page #	text only	30% art	70% art
1			
2			
3			
4			
5			
6			
7			
8			
9			
10			
11			
12			
13			
14			
15			

	Page Printing Time (seconds)		
Page #	text only	30% art	70% art
16			
17			
18			
19			
20			
21			
22			
23			
24			
25			
26			
27			
28			
29			
30			

Total # Pages	text only	30% art	70% art

Total Print Time	text only	30% art	70% art

Average Printing Time at	text only	30% art	70% art

By collecting and averaging a number of sample points, these models become machine standards for your shop. This data collection process works for each input or output device in your business.

II. Operator Standards

Measurement Units

Below are common measurement units for defining the typical performance rates of desktop system operators. These "accepted industry standards" are based on research by associations, professional groups and our own extensive survey.

FUNCTION	MEASUREMENT
Keyboarding	Characters per time unit Words per minute
Editing	1,000 characters per minute
Proofreading	1,000 characters per minute
Scanning	Minutes per scan
Scan retouch	Minutes per image (based on various sizes and complexities)
Color editing	Minutes per image (based on various sizes and complexities)
Typography	Characters per time unit
Design	Minutes/hours per page (based on size and complexity)
Layout	Minutes/hours per page (based on size and complexity)

NAPL Production Standards The National Association of Printers and Lithographers developed a *Cost Study on
Desktop/Electronic Publishing Operations*. Non-members can
purchase this study from the NAPL for $100. (Members pay
$50).

The following is a synopsis of the NAQP analysis for individual (first time) operations. Subsequent operations can take
slightly less time.

Operation	Measurement	Comments
Keyboarding	4.8 min/1000 char	12,500/hr - straight text
Proofreading	2 min/1000 char	30/hr - non-technical text
B&W Scanning (halftones)	14 min/scan	4.3 scans/hr - up to 8 x 10 incl setup, scan, preview, adjustments, name & save file
B&W Scanning (line art)	10 min/scan	6 scans/hr - up to 8 x 10 incl setup, scan, preview, adjustments, name & save file
Color Scanning	33 min/scan	1.8 scans/hr - up to 8 x 10 incl setup, scan, preview, adjustments, name & save file
Color Editing	25 min/image	2.4 images/hr - med quality incl setup, scan, preview, adjustments, name & save file
Composition/ Layout (text) (non-process)	15 min/pg	4 pg/hr - setup, importing text, composition, pagina tion, adjust for non-process color

Operation	Measurement	Comments
Composition/ Layout (text & graphics) (non-process)	26 min/pg	2.3 pg/hr - setup, import txt & graphics, add tints, composition, pagination, adjustments for non-process color pages
Composition/ Layout (text & graphics) (process color)	42 min/pg	1.4 pg/hr - setup, import txt & graphics, add tints, composition, pagination, adjustments for process color pages
Trapping	26 min/pg	2.3/hr - setup, EPS file, display pg, check color traps, adjust as necessary
Laser Print B&W Proof	1.5 min/pg	40 pg/hr - downloading text fonts & graphics, RIPing, and imaging
Color Proofs Proof	3 min/pg	20 pg/hr - downloading text fonts & graphics, low res color RIPing, imaging
Imagesetting Final output	4 min/film	15 films/hr - text & graphics. Incl download fonts, RIPing, imaging, developing film
Blueline & Dyluxes (final proof)	9 min/flat	6.7 flats/hr - setup, vacuum frame, exposing, development trimming
Matchprint & Chromalin (final proof)	36 min/flat	1.7 flats/hr - setup, vacuum frame, exposing, development laminating, trimming

A complete copy of the NAPL industry standards can be purchased by contacting them at 780 Palisade Avenue, Teaneck, NJ 07666 (201/342-0700).

NASS Production Standards The National Association of Secretarial Services also developed a timing standard for their industry. They call their special report: *Industry Production Standards - Guidelines for Business Support Providers.*

Here's a sampling of the NASS timing standards for individual (first time) operations. Subsequent operations can take slightly less time.

Operation	Measurement
General Keyboarding	70 words/minute
Word Processing	
single-spaced pages	15 minutes/page
double-spaced pages	7.5 minutes/page
names & addresses from list	100 addresses/hr
print merged letters (1 page)	1 minute/letter
print 3" x 15/16" labels	500 labels/hour
Desktop Publishing	
base time unit	12 min/page plus attributes
Attribute:	add for each occurrence:
each column	6 minutes/page
each font over 3 fonts/pg	6 minutes/page
each tab setting	6 minutes/page
each type of bullet	6 minutes/page
each type of line	6 minutes/page
each type of Dingbat	6 minutes/page
each boxed element	6 minutes/page
each reverse	6 minutes/page
each shaded area	6 minutes/page
each line art placed	6 minutes/page
each color illustration	6 minutes/page
each photo placed	6 minutes/page

A complete copy of the NASS industry standards can be purchased by contacting them at 3637 Fourth Street North, Suite 330, St. Petersburg, FL 33704 (813/823-3646).

BIG Operator Performance "Standards" Every 12 to
14 months,our company conducts an extensive survey to collect
pricing information covering desktop publishing and prepress
operations. Over 26,000 businesses are invited to participate in
the confidential survey.

Some owners respond by listing hourly rates. Others list
prices by the job, by the piece, or by the page. When both hourly
rates and task prices are provided, we can calculate a rough time
value for each operation. By removing gross profit (assumed
10%), these numbers provide a good relative representation of
how long it takes to perform specific tasks. There is a close
correlation between our operator performance times and industry
production standards published by other organizations.

The next several pages list operator performance times based
on survey responses. When minimum charges were provided
with an accompanying hourly rate, these were interpreted to be
charges for the simplest job in that task category. Gross profit
has been removed making these values a good approximation of
real performance time.

Key to Data Units

cph = characters per hour

files/hr = files per hour

hr ea = hours each

hr/job = hours per job

hr/pc = hours per piece

hr/pkg - hours per package

hr/set = hours per set

min = minutes

min/pg = minutes per page

pg/hr = pages per hour

scans/hr = scans per hour

sec/file = seconds per file

BIG Operator Performance Times
(based on survey database)

Input Processes

WRITING
Converting concept into legible, grammatically correct text; save as word processing file.

General Copy	Simple	Complex	Average
	7.6 pg/hr	0.2 pg/hr	1.7 pg/hr
	7 min/pg	374 min/pg	35 min/pg
Newsletter Copy	Simple	Complex	Average
	7.3 pg/hr	0.2 pg/hr	1.3 pg/hr
	8 min/pg	263 min/pg	48 min/pg
PR & Advertising	Simple	Complex	Average
	7.1 pg/hr	0.1 pg/hr	1.2 pg/hr
	8.3 min/pg	545 min/pg	50 min/pg
Resumes	Simple	Complex	Average
	5.5 pg/hr	0.4 pg/hr	1.3 pg/hr
	11 min/pg	17 min/pg	50 min/pg
Technical	Simple	Complex	Average
	2.1 pg/hr	0.2 pg/hr	0.4 pg/hr
	33 min/pg	40 min/pg	100 min/pg

KEYBOARDING
Converting rough notes into 10-12 point type, save as data file. (cph = characters per hour) (pg/hr = pages per hour)

Data Entry	Simple	Complex	Average
	28,938 cph	2,056 cph	10,801 cph
	5.63 pg/hr	1.7 pg/hr	7.7 pg/hr
	3 min/pg	33 min/pg	8 min/pg

KEYBOARDING (cont'd.)

Word Processing	Simple	Complex	Average
(70 wpm speed)	15.8 pg/hr	5.8 pg/hr	9.7 pg/hr
	3.8 min/pg	10.3 min/pg	6.2 min/pg

NOTE; A recent article in *Imaging Magazine* compared data entry times for manual keying, OCR and bar code. For a 20-character data field the folloiwng times are representative:

Manual keying	10 seconds/20 characters
OCR	4 seconds/20 characters
Bar Code	4 seconds/20 characters

EDITING & PROOFREADING

Careful, line-by-line check and proofread, hand markup draft or edit on customer's disk (no retype).

General Copy	Simple	Complex	Average
	15.4 pg/hr	2.2 pg/hr	12.9 pg/hr
	3.9 min/pg	27.3 min/pg	4.7 min/pg

EDITING

Careful check for accuracy and flow, hand markup draft or edit on customer's disk (no retype).

Content Editing	Simple	Complex	Average
	12.8 pg/hr	2.8 pg/hr	10.8 pg/hr
	4.7 min/pg	21.4 min/pg	5.6 min/pg
Copy Editing			400 words/hour

TYPOGRAPHY

Apply styles, typefaces & fonts to text file, arrange into pages, spell check and save as file.

General	Simple	Complex	Average
	13.8 pg/hr	0.7 pg/hr	3 pg/hr
	4.3 min/pg	85.7 min/pg	20 min/pg
Resume	Simple	Complex	Average
	5.5 pg/hr	0.84 pg/hr	1.14 pg/hr
	10.9 min/pg	71.4 min/pg	53 min/pg

TYPOGRAPHY (cont'd.)

Tables	Simple	Complex	Average
	6.9 pg/hr	0.4 pg/hr	2.5 pg/hr
	8.7 min/pg	150 min/pg	24 min/pg

TRANSCRIPTION

General	(0.3 minutes/word)

TRANSLATION

General	(36 minutes/100 words)
Engl --> Spanish	0.36 minutes/word
Other International	(1.54 hours/page)

FILE CONVERSION

Convert from one file format to another (e.g., 123 to Excel, Word PC to Word Macintosh).

File-to-File	Simple	Complex	Average
	5.5 files/hr	1.5 files/hr	4.2 files/hr
	10.9 min/file	40 min/file	14.3 min/file

SCAN INPUT

Scan image, minimal edit retouch, convert into PICT, TIFF format, save as file.

BW Line Art	Simple	Complex	Average
	13.0 scans/hr	4.0 scans/hr	5.4 scans/hr
	4.6 min/scan	15 min/scan	11.1 min/scan
BW Gray Scale	Simple	Complex	Average
	12.8 scans/hr	4.0 scans/hr	5.4 scans/hr
	4.7 min/scan	15.0 min/scan	11.1 min/scan
BW Photo	Simple	Complex	Average
	12.8 scans/hr	4.0 scans/hr	5.3 scans/hr
	4.7 min/scan	15.0 min/scan	11.3 min/scan
Color Illustration	Simple	Complex	Average
	12.6 scans/hr	3.9 scans/hr	5.2 scans/hr
	4.8 min/scan	15.4 min/scan	11.5 min/scan

SCANNING (cont'd.)

Color Photo	Simple	Complex	Average
	12.7 scans/hr	3.9 scans/hr	5.2 scans/hr
	4.7 min/scan	154 min/scan	11.5 min/scan

SCAN INPUT (OCR)

Scan page, spell check scanned text, save as word processing file.

OCR Text	Simple	Complex	Average
	42.3 pg/hr	2.9 pg/hr	6.0 pg/hr
	1.4 min/pg	20.7 min/pg	10 min/pg

Creative Design

COMPUTER GENERATED ART

Converting concept or rough draft into computer graphic, save as file.

Computer Art	Simple	Complex	Average
	0.5 hr ea	3 hr ea	1.2 hr ea
	30 min ea	180 min ea	72 min ea

ILLUSTRATION

Converting concept or rough draft into graphic image, save as file.

Illustration	Simple	Complex	Average
	0.3 hr ea	3.5 hr ea	1.4 hr ea
	18 min ea	210 min ea	84 min ea

LOGO DESIGN

Converting concept or rough draft into stand-alone graphic image, save as file, design includes two comps with minor modifications to the one chosen.

Logo	Simple	Complex	Average
	2.1 hr ea	14.9 hr ea	6.8 hr ea
	126 min ea	894 min ea	408 min ea

LOGOTYPE DESIGN

Convert concept or rough draft into custom typography or lettering, render as stand-alone graphic image, save as file.

Logotype	Simple	Complex	Average
	0.2 hr ea	17 hr ea	5.2 hr ea
	12 min ea	1020 min ea	312 min ea

Page Layout

ANNOUNCEMENTS

Convert concept or rough draft into electronic page, import and place graphics, design and layout as 8.5 x 11, 2 to 4 up page, simple one color to complex four color, save as file.

	Simple	Complex	Average
Text Only	0.4 hr ea	1.2 hr ea	0.7 hr ea
	24 min ea	72 min ea	39 min ea
Text w/Graphics	0.6 hr ea	1.7 hr ea	0.75 hr ea
	36 min ea	102 min ea	45 min ea

ANNUAL REPORTS

Convert concept or rough draft into electronic page, import and place graphics, design and layout as 8.5 x 11 page, simple one color to complex four color, save as file.

	Simple	Complex	Average
Text Only	0.2 hr/pg	8.1 hr/pg	1.6 hr/pg
	12 min/pg	486 min/pg	96 min/pg
Text w/Graphics	0.6 hr/pg	9.1 hr/pg	1.6 hr/pg
	36 min/pg	546 min/pg	108 min/pg
Job - Text Only	2.2 hr/job	72.7 hr/job	17.6 hr/job
Job - w/Graphics	2.7 hr/job	261.8 hr/job	65.2 hr/job

BOOK COVER

Convert concept or rough draft into electronic page, import and place graphics, design and layout as simple one color to complex four color, save as page layout file.

	Simple	Complex	Average
Text Only	0.2 hr ea	12.1 hr ea	3.9 hr ea
	12 min ea	726 min ea	234 min ea
Text w/Graphics	0.3 hr ea	46.8 hr ea	10.8 hr ea
	18 min ea	2808 min ea	648 min ea

BOOK INTERIOR

Convert concept or rough draft into electronic page, import and place graphics, design and layout as simple one color to complex four color, save as page layout file.

	Simple	Complex	Average
Text Only	0.1 hr/pg	0.5 hr/pg	0.3 hr/pg
	6 min/pg	30 min/pg	18 min/pg
	10 pg/hr	2.0 pg/hr	3.3 pg/hr
Text w/Graphics	0.3 hr/pg	0.7 hr/pg	0.6 hr/pg
	18 min/pg	42 min/pg	36 min/pg
	3.3 pg/hr	1.4 pg/hr	1.7 pg/hr

BOOK JACKET

Convert concept or rough draft into jacket-size electronic page, import and place graphics, design and layout as simple one color to complex four color, save as page layout file.

	Simple	Complex	Average
Text Only	0.9 hr ea	15.8 hr ea	7.6 hr ea
	54 min ea	948 min ea	456 min ea
Text w/Graphics	1 hr ea	26 hr ea	12.2 hr ea
	60 min ea	1560 min ea	732 min ea

BOOKLETS

Convert concept or rough draft into electronic booklet-size pages, import and place text/graphics, design and layout as simple one color to complex four color, save as file.

	Simple	Complex	Average
Text Only	0.2 hr/pg 10.7 min/pg 5.6 pg/hr	2.5 hr/pg 150 min/pg 0.4 pg/hr	1.1 hr/pg 66.7 min/pg 0.9 pg/hr
Text w/Graphics	0.27 hr/pg 16.2 min/pg 3.7 pg/hr	3.3 hr/pg 198 min/pg 0.3 pg/hr	1.25 hr/pg 75 min/pg 0.8 pg/hr
Job - Text Only	0.4 hr/job	14.6 hr/job	3.1 hr/job
Job - w/Graphics	0.6 hr/job	27.3 hr/job	5.8 hr/job

BROCHURE

Convert concept or rough draft into electronic 8.5 x 11, tri-fold (6-panel) 3 panels per side pages, import and place text/graphics, design and layout as simple one color to complex four color, save as page layout file.

	Simple	Complex	Average
Text Only	0.4 hr/pg 24 min/pg	2.29 hr/pg 137.4 min/pg	1.4 hr/pg 84 min/pg
Text w/Graphics	0.5 hr/pg 30 min/pg	3.3 hr/pg 198 min/pg	1.9 hr/pg 114 min/pg
Job - Text Only	2 hr/job	15.2 hr/job	5.3 hr/job
Job - w/Graphics	2.3 hr/job	19.5 hr/job	8.6 hr/job

BULLETIN

Convert concept or rough draft into electronic page, import and place graphics, design and layout as 8.5 x 11 page, simple one color to complex four color, save as page layout file.

	Simple	Complex	Average
Text Only	0.3 hr/pg 18 min/pg	4.6 hr/pg 276 min/pg	1 hr/pg 60 min/pg

BULLETIN

w/Graphics	0.8 hr/pg	6.4 hr/pg	1.9 hr/pg
	48 min/pg	384 min/pg	114 min/pg

BUSINESS STATIONERY

Convert concept or rough draft into electronic page, import and place graphics, design and layout envelope, letterhead and business card as 8.5 x 11 pages, simple one color to complex four color, save as page layout file.

	Simple	Complex	Average
Text or graphics	0.7 hr/set	9.1 hr/set	2.9 hr/set

CALENDAR

Convert concept or rough draft into electronic page, import and place graphics, design and layout as 8.5 x 11 pages, simple one color to complex four color, save as file.

	Simple	Complex	Average
Text Only	0.3 hr/pg	1.8 hr/pg	1 hr/pg
	20 min/pg	108 min/pg	60 min/pg
	3 pg/hr	0.6 pg/hr	1 pg/hr
w/Graphics	0.7 hr/pg	2.02 hr/pg	1.32 hr/pg
	42 min/pg	120 min/pg	78 min/pg
	1.5 pg/hr	0.5 pg/hr	0.8 pg/hr
Job	4.8 hr/job	7.6 hr/job	6.2 hr/job

CARD (BUSINESS)

Convert concept or rough draft into electronic page, import and place graphics, design and layout as 8.5 x 11 page, 10-up, simple one color to complex four color, save as file.

	Simple	Complex	Average
Text Only	0.4 hr/pg	3.1 hr/pg	0.9 hr/pg
	24 min/pg	186 min/pg	54 min/pg
w/Graphics	.5 hr/pg	3.3 hr/pg	.8 hr/pg
	30 min/pg	198 min/pg	48 min/pg

CARD (BUSINESS REPLY)

Convert concept or rough draft into electronic page, import and place graphics, design and layout as 8.5 x 11 page, 1- or 2-up, 2-side, simple 1 color to complex 4 color, save as file.

	Simple	Complex	Average
Text Only	0.4 hrs ea 23 min ea	1.8 hrs ea 109 min ea	0.9 hrs ea 52 min ea
w/Graphics	1 hr ea 58 min ea	2.2 hrs ea 133 min ea	1.4 hrs ea 84 min ea

CARD (FOLDOVER)

Convert concept or rough draft into electronic page, import and place graphics, design and layout as 8.5 x 11 page, 1- or 2-up, 2-side, simple 1 color to complex 4 color, save as file.

	Simple	Complex	Average
Text Only	0.4 hrs ea 23 min ea	1 hr ea 60 min ea	0.6 hrs ea 37 min ea
w/Graphics	0.5 hrs ea 30 min ea	1.4 hrs ea 82 min ea	0.9 hrs ea 51 min ea

CARD (GREETING)

Convert concept or rough draft into electronic page, import and place graphics, design and layout as 2-side card, simple one color to complex four color, save as page layout file.

	Simple	Complex	Average
Text w/Graphics	1 hr ea 60 min ea	2 hrs ea 120 min ea	1.5 hrs ea 90 min ea

CARD (ROTARY)

Convert concept or rough draft into electronic page, import and place text/graphics, design and layout as 8.5 x 11 page, simple one color to four color (complex), save as file.

	Simple	Complex	Average
Text Only	0.3 hrs ea 16 min ea	1.1 hrs ea 68 min ea	0.9 hrs ea 41 min ea
w/Graphics	0.5 hrs ea 31 min ea	1.4 hrs ea 82 min ea	0.9 hrs ea 56 min ea

CARTOON

Convert concept or rough draft into electronic page, import and place text/graphics, design and layout as 8.5 x 11 page, simple one color to four color (complex), save as file.

	Simple	Complex	Average
Graphic	0.1 hrs ea	6.4 hrs ea	2.3 hrs ea
	6 min ea	384 min ea	138 min ea

CATALOG

Convert concept or rough draft into electronic page, import and place text/graphics, design and layout as pages, simple one color to four color (complex), save as file.

	Simple	Complex	Average
Text Only	0.4 hr/pg	14.2 hr/pg	1.7 hr/pg
	24 min/pg	148.5 min/pg	103 min/pg
	2.7 pg/hr	0.4 pg/hr	0.7 pg/hr
w/Graphics	0.7 hr/pg	5.0 hr/pg	2.5 hr/pg
	42 min/pg	300 min/pg	150 min/pg
	1.4 pg/hr	0.2 pg/hr	0.4 pg/hr

CERTIFICATE

Convert concept or rough draft into electronic page, import and place text/graphics, design and layout as 8.5 x 11 page, simple one color to four color (complex), save as file.

	Simple	Complex	Average
Text Only	0.2 hrs ea	2.0 hrs ea	1.0 hrs ea
	12 min ea	120 min ea	60 min ea
w/Graphics	0.2 hrs ea	3 hrs ea	0.8 hrs ea
	8 min ea	182 min ea	49 min ea

CHARTS/DIAGRAMS

Convert concept or rough draft into electronic page, import and place text/graphics, design and layout as 8.5 x 11 page, simple one color to four color (complex), save as file.

	Simple	Complex	Average
Text Only	0.3 hrs ea	1.4 hrs ea	0.8 hrs ea
	18 min ea	84 min ea	48 min ea

CHARTS/DIAGRAMS (contd)

w/Graphics	0.6 hrs ea	2.7 hrs ea	1.1 hrs ea
	36 min ea	162 min ea	66 min ea

DIRECT MAIL PACKAGE

Convert concept or rough draft into electronic pages, import and place text/graphics, design and layout as 8.5 x 11 pages, simple one color to four color (complex), save as file.

	Simple	Complex	Average
Piece	0.9 hr/pc	2 hr/pc	2 hr/pc
	54 min/pc	120 min/pc	120 min/pc
	1.1 pcs/hr	5 pcs/hr	0.5 pcs/hr
	Simple	Complex	Average
Job	3.3 hr/job	40.9 hr/job	15.2 hr/job

DIRECTORY

Convert concept or rough draft into electronic pages, import and place text/graphics, design and layout as 8.5 x 11 pages, simple one color to four color (complex), save as file.

	Simple	Complex	Average
Text Only	0.2 hr/pg	1.7 hr/pg	0.7 hr/pg
	12 min/pg	102 min/pg	42 min/pg
	6.3 pg/hr	0.6 pg/hr	1.5 pg/hr
w/Graphics	0.2 hr/pg	2.0 hr/pg	0.8 hr/pg
	12 min/pg	120 min/pg	48 min/pg
	4.4 pg/hr	0.5 pg/hr	1.3 pg/hr
Job	16.2 hr/job	26.8 hr/job	17.9 hr/job

DISPLAY AD

Convert concept or rough draft into electronic page, import and place text/graphics, design/layout as 8.5 x 11 page with crop marks, simple 1 color to 4 color (complex), save as file.

	Simple	Complex	Average
Text Only	0.5 hrs ea	2.7 hrs ea	1.5 hrs ea
	30 min ea	162 min ea	90 min ea
w/Graphics	7.8 hr ea	13.9 hrs ea	10.6 hrs ea
	468 min ea	834 min ea	636 min ea

DOOR HANGER

Convert concept or rough draft into electronic page, import and place text/graphics, design and layout as 8.5 x 11, 2-up page, simple one color to four color (complex), save as file.

	Simple	Complex	Average
Text Only	0.2 hrs ea	1.1 hrs ea	0.7 hrs ea
	12 min ea	66 min ea	42 min ea
w/Graphics	0.4 hrs ea	2.1 hrs ea	1.1 hrs ea
	24 min ea	126 min ea	66 min ea

FLYER

Convert concept or rough draft into electronic page, import and place text/graphics, design and layout as 8.5 x 11 page, simple one color to four color (complex), save as file.

	Simple	Complex	Average
Text Only	0.6 hrs ea	1.0 hrs ea	.7 hr ea
	36 min ea	60 min ea	42 min ea
w/Graphics	0.5 hrs ea	3.2 hrs ea	.9 hrs ea
	30 min ea	192 min ea	54 min ea

FORM

Convert concept or rough draft into electronic page, import and place text/graphics, design and layout as 8.5 x 11 page, simple one color to four color (complex), save as file.

	Simple	Complex	Average
Text Only	0.3 hrs ea	2.7 hrs ea	1.1 hrs ea
	18 min ea	162 min ea	66 min ea
w/Graphics	0.6 hrs ea	3.7 hrs ea	1.5 hrs ea
	36 min ea	222 min ea	90 min ea

HANDBOOK

Convert concept or rough draft into electronic page, import and place text/graphics, design and layout as 8.5 x 11 page, simple one color, standard format with no major tables to complex four color with tables, save as file.

	Simple	Complex	Average
Text Only	0.2 hr/pg	1.7 hr/pg	0.9 hr/pg
	12 min/pg	102 min/pg	54 min/pg
	5 pg/hr	0.6 pg/hr	1.1 pg/hr

HANDBOOK (contd)

w/Graphics	0.3 hr/pg	1.4 hr/pg	0.8 hr/pg
	18 min/pg	84 min/pg	48 min/pg
	3.2 pg/hr	0.7 pg/hr	1.2 pg/hr

INSERT

Convert concept or rough draft into electronic page, import and place text/graphics, design/layout as 8.5 x 11 page, simple 1 color, standard format with no major text/graphics to complex 4 color with text and difficult graphics, save as file.

	Simple	Complex	Average
Text Only	0.4 hr/pg	1 hr/pg	0.7 hr/pg
	24 min/pg	60 min/pg	42 min/pg
w/Graphics	0.5 hr/pg	3.2 hr/pg	1.4 hr/pg
	30 min/pg	192 min/pg	84 min/pg

INVITATION

Convert concept or rough draft into electronic page, import and place text/graphics, design and layout as 8.5 x 11 page with crop marks, simple one color to complex four color with text and difficult graphics, save as file.

	Simple	Complex	Average
Text Only	0.4 hr/pg	1.9 hr/pg	1.1 hr/pg
	24 min/pg	114 min/pg	66 min/pg
w/Graphics	0.5 hr/pg	2.4 hr/pg	1.2 hr/pg
	30 min/pg	144 min/pg	72 min/pg

LABEL (CUSTOM)

Convert concept or rough draft into electronic page, import and place text/graphics, design and layout as 8.5 x 11, 4- to 33-up page, simple 1 color to complex 4 color, save as file.

	Simple	Complex	Average
Text Only	0.4 hr/pg	1.8 hr/pg	0.8 hr/pg
	24 min/pg	108 min/pg	48 min/pg
w/Graphics	0.6 hr/pg	2.7 hr/pg	1.6 hr/pg
	36 min/pg	162 min/pg	96 min/pg

LETTERHEAD & ENVELOPE

Converting concept or rough draft into electronic page, import and place graphics, design and layout as simple one color to complex four color, save as page layout file.

	Simple	Complex	Average
Text Only	0.5 hr/set	4.6 hr/set	1.0 hr/set
	30 min/set	276 min/set	60 min/set
w/Graphics	0.6 hr/set	2.7 hr/set	1.6 hr/set
	36 min/set	162 min/set	96 min/set

MAGAZINE

Convert concept or rough draft into electronic page, import and place text/graphics, design and layout as 8.5 x 11 pages, simple one color to complex four color, save as file.

	Simple	Complex	Average
Text Only	0.2 hr/pg	1.4 hr/pg	1.0 hr/pg
	12.4 min/pg	84 min/pg	60 min/pg
	4.8 pg/hr	0.7 pg/hr	1 pg/hr
w/Graphics	0.3 hr/pg	3.3 hr/pg	1.25 hr/pg
	18 min/pg	198 min/pg	75 min/pg
	3.2 pg/hr	0.3 pg/hr	0.8 pg/hr
Job	11.36 hr/job	72.8 hr/job	66.3 hr/job

MANUAL

Convert concept or rough draft into electronic pages, import and place text/graphics, design and layout as 8.5 x 11 pages, simple one color to complex four color, save as file.

	Simple	Complex	Average
Text Only	0.2 hr/pg	1.4 hr/pg	0.6 hr/pg
	14 min/pg	82 min/pg	37 min/pg
	4.4 pg/hr	0.7 pg/hr	1.6 pg/hr
w/Graphics	0.3 hr/pg	4.6 hr/pg	0.9 hr/pg
	14 min/pg	273 min/pg	55 min/pg
	4.2 pg/hr	0.2 pg/hr	1.1 pg/hr
Job	1.8 hr/job	41.6 hr/job	16.5 hr/job

MAP

Convert concept or rough draft into electronic page, import and place text/graphics, design and layout as 8.5 x 11 page, simple one color to complex four color, save as file.

	Simple	Complex	Average
One Sheet	0.5 hrs ea	68.2 hrs ea	9.4 hrs ea
	30 min ea	4,092 min ea	564 min ea

MEMO / NOTE PAD

Convert concept or rough draft into electronic page, import and place text/graphics, design and layout as 8.5 x 11, 2-up page, simple one color to complex four color, save as file.

	Simple	Complex	Average
Text Only	0.2 hr/pg	0.9 hr/pg	0.5 hr/pg
	12 min//pg	54 min/pg	30 min/pg
w/Graphics	0.3 hr/pg	1.8 hr/pg	0.8 hr/pg
	18 min/pg	108 min/pg	48 min/pg

MENU

Convert concept or rough draft into electronic page, import and place text/graphics, design and layout as 8.5 x 11 page, simple one color to complex four color, save as file.

	Simple	Complex	Average
Text Only	0.5 hr/pg	3 hr/pg	1.2 hr/pg
	30 min/pg	180 min/pg	72 min/pg
w/Graphics	0.6 hr/pg	3.6 hr/pg	1.7 hr/pg
	36 min/pg	216 min/pg	102 min/pg
Job - Text	0.81 hr/job	10.9 hr/job	4.5 hr/job
Job - w/Graphics	0.9 hr/job	26.7 hr/job	6.8 hr/job

NEWSLETTER

Convert concept or rough draft into electronic page, import and place text/graphics, design and layout as 2- or 3-column, 8.5 x 11 page, simple 1 color to complex 4 color, save as file.

	Simple	Complex	Average
Text Only	0.4 hr/pg	3.3 hr/pg	.7 hr/pg
	24 min/pg	198 min/pg	42 min/pg
	2.6 pg/hr	0.3 pg/hr	1.4 pg/hr

NEWSLETTER (contd)

w/Graphics	0.4 hr/pg	3.3 hr/pg	0.7 hr/pg
	24 min/pg	198 min/pg	42 min/pg
	2.6 pg/hr	0.3 pg/hr	1.4 pg/hr
Job - Text	2.12 hr/job	20.2 hr/job	5.57 hr/job
Job - w/Graphics	2.63 hr/job	30.4 hr/job	8.17 hr/job

PACKAGING

Convert concept or rough draft into electronic page, import and place text/graphics, design and layout as simple one color to complex four color pages, save as file.

	Simple	Complex	Average
Package	0.9 hr/pkg	27.3 hr/pkg	11.6 hr/pkg
	54 min/pkg	1,638 min/pkg	696 min/pkg

POST CARD (CUSTOM)

Convert concept or rough draft into electronic page, import and place text/graphics, design and layout as 2- to 4-up, 8.5 x 11 page, simple one color to complex four color; save as file.

	Simple	Complex	Average
Text Only	0.4 hrs ea	3.7 hrs ea	0.9 hrs ea
	24 min ea	222 min ea	54 min ea
w/Graphics	0.4 hrs ea	3.8 hrs ea	11.3 hrs ea
	24 min ea	228 min ea	678 min ea

POSTER

Convert concept or rough draft into electronic page, import and place text/graphics, design and layout as 8.5 x 11 page, simple one color to complex four color; save as file.

	Simple	Complex	Average
Text Only	0.31 hrs ea	6.8 hrs ea	2.45 hrs ea
	19 min ea	408 min ea	147 min ea
w/Graphics	0.51 hrs ea	13.6 hrs ea	4.89 hrs ea
	31 min ea	816 min ea	293 min ea

PRESENTATION DESIGN

Convert concept or rough draft into electronic pages, import and place text/graphics, design and layout as 8.5 x 11 pages, simple one color to complex four color; save as file.

	Simple	Complex	Average
Text Only	0.3 hr/pg	0.8 hr/pg	0.5 hr/pg
	18 min/pg	48 min/pg	30 min/pg
w/Graphics	0.4 hr/pg	2.1 hr/pg	1 hr/pg
	24 min/pg	126 min/pg	60 min/pg

PRICE LIST

Convert concept or rough draft into electronic pages, import and place text/graphics, design and layout as 8.5 x 11 pages, simple one color to complex four color; save as file.

	Simple	Complex	Average
Text Only	0.3 hr/pg	2.3 hr/pg	1 hr/pg
	18 min/pg	138 min/pg	60 min/pg
w/Graphics	0.5 hr/pg	2.4 hr/pg	1.5 hr/pg
	30 min/pg	144 min/pg	90 min/pg

PRINT AD

Convert concept or rough draft into electronic page, import and place text/graphics, design and layout as 8.5 x 11 page, simple one color to complex four color; save as file.

	Simple	Complex	Average
Text Only	0.3 hrs ea	6.8 hrs ea	1.9 hrs ea
	18 min/pg	408 min/pg	114 min/pg
w/Graphics	0.46 hrs ea	9.09 hrs ea	2.54 hrs ea
	27.6 min/pg	545 min/pg	152 min/pg

PROCEDURE GUIDE

Convert concept or rough draft into electronic pages, import and place text/graphics, design and layout as 8.5 x 11 pages, simple one color to complex four color; save as file.

	Simple	Complex	Average
Text Only	0.3 hr/pg	0.8 hr/pg	0.6 hr/pg
	18 min/pg	48 min/pg	36 min/pg
	3.3 pg/hr	1.2 pg/hr	1.8 pg/hr

PROCEDURE GUIDE (contd)

w/Graphics	0.5 hr/pg	0.9 hr/pg	0.7 hr/pg
	30 min/pg	54 min/pg	42 min/pg
	2 pg/hr	1.1 pg/hr	1.4 pg/hr

PRODUCT LITERATURE

Convert concept or rough draft into electronic pages, import and place text/graphics, design and layout as 8.5 x 11 pages, simple one color to complex four color; save as file.

	Simple	Complex	Average
Text Only	0.32 hr/pg	1.1 hr/pg	0.8 hr/pg
	19 min/pg	66 min/pg	48 min/pg
	3.1 pg/hr	0.9 pg/hr	1.2 pg/hr
w/Graphics	0.5 hr/pg	2.5 hr/pg	1.4 hr/pg
	30 min/pg	150 min/pg	84 min/pg
	2 pg/hr	0.4 pg/hr	0.7 pg/hr
Job - Text	2.12 hr/job	6.49 hr/job	4.38 hr/job.
Job - w/Graphics	4.54 hr/job	19.48 hr/job	9.69 hr/job

Operation   Survey Measurement

PRODUCT SPECIFICATION SHEET

Convert concept or rough draft into electronic page, import and place text/graphics, design and layout as 8.5 x 11 page, simple one color to complex four color; save as file.

	Simple	Complex	Average
Text Only	0.3 hr/pg	1.1 hr/pg	0.7 hr/pg
	18 min/pg	66 min/pg	42 min/pg
	3.3 pg/hr	0.9 pg/hr	1.4 pg/hr
w/Graphics	0.5 hr/pg	1.25 hr/pg	0.8 hr/pg
	30 min/pg	75 min/pg	48 min/pg
	2 hr/pg	0.8 hr/pg	1.2 hr/pg
Job - Text	4.1 hr/job	6.5 hr/job	5.5 hr/job
Job - w/Graphics	4.5 hr/job	16.2 hr/job	10 hr/job

PROGRAM

Convert concept or rough draft into electronic page, import and place text/graphics, design and layout as 8.5 x 11 page (one fold), simple 1 color to complex 4 color; save as file.

Text Only	Simple	Complex	Average
	0.2 hr/pg	5 hr/pg	1 hr/pg
	12 min/pg	300 min/pg	60 min/pg
	5.6 pg/hr	0.2 pg/hr	1 pg/hr
w/Graphics	0.27 hr/pg	5.0 hr/pg	1.25 hr/pg
	16 min/pg	300 min/pg	75 min/pg
	3.7 hr/pg	0.2 hr/pg	0.8 hr/pg

RESUME

Typically 1 page provided on hard copy, simple 1 to 4 color (complex), save as file. Some shops provide up to 25 copies with matching envelopes and 25 extra blank sheets for cover letter, Disk with resume file may be provided at extra cost. .

Text Only	Simple	Complex	Average
	0.1 hrs ea	3.1 hrs ea	0.9 hrs ea
	6 min ea	186 min ea	54 min ea

SIGNAGE

Convert concept or rough draft into electronic page, import and place text/graphics, design and layout as 8.5 x 11 page, simple one color to complex four color; save as file.

Text Only	Simple	Complex	Average
	0.5 hr/pg	7.6 hr/pg	2.8 hr/pg
	30 min/pg	454 min/pg	168 min/pg

SLIDE DESIGN

Convert concept or rough draft into electronic page, import and place text/graphics, design and layout as 8.5 x 11 page, simple one color to complex four color; save as file.

Text Only	Simple	Complex	Average
	0.3 hrs ea	0.9 hrs ea	0.6 hrs ea
	18 min ea	54 min ea	36 min ea
w/Graphics	0.5 hrs ea	1 hrs ea	0.7 hrs ea
	30 min ea	60 min ea	42 min ea

TABLOID

Convert concept or rough draft into electronic page, import and place text/graphics, design and layout as 11 x 17 page, simple one color to complex four color; save as file.

	Simple	Complex	Average
Text Only	0.77 hr/pg	3.3 hr/pg	1.7 hr/pg
	46.2 min/pg	198 min/pg	102 min/pg
	1.3 pg/hr	0.3 pg/hr	0.6 pg/hr
w/Graphics	1.4 hr/pg	3.3 hr/pg	2.0 hr/pg
	84 min/pg	198 min/pg	120 min/pg
	0.7 pg/hr	0.3 pg/hr	0.5 pg/hr
Job - Text	2. hr/job	7.9 hr/job	5.6 hr/job

TICKETS

Convert concept or rough draft into electronic page, import and place text/graphics, design and layout as 4- to 18-up 8.5 x 11 page, simple one color to complex four color; save as file.

	Simple	Complex	Average
Text Only	0.2 hr/pg	1.2 hr/pg	0.6 hr/pg
	12 min/pg	72 min/pg	36 min/pg
w/Graphics	0.4 hr/pg	1.3 hr/pg	0.8 hr/pg
	24 min/pg	78 min/pg	48 min/pg

TRANSPARENCY (BW)

Convert concept or rough draft into electronic page, import and place text/graphics, design and layout as 8.5 x 11 page with crop marks, simple text only to complex text/graphics image; save as file.

	Simple	Complex	Average
Text Only	0.1 hr ea	1.6 hr ea	0.6 hr ea
	6 min ea	96 min ea	36 min ea
w/Graphics	0.4 hr ea	3 hr ea	1.1 hr ea
	24 min ea	180 min ea	66 min ea

TRANSPARENCY (COLOR)

Convert concept or rough draft into electronic page, import and place text/graphics, design and layout as 8.5 x 11 page with crop marks, simple one color to complex 4C text/graphics image; save as file.

	Simple	Complex	Average
Text Only	0.3 hr ea	1.6 hr ea	0.7 hr ea
	18 min ea	96 min ea	42 min ea
w/Graphics	0.5 hrs ea	3.1 hrs ea	1.4 hrs ea
	30 min ea	186 min ea	84 min ea

Output Processes

DOCUMENT IMAGING

Convert text into computer data, save on tape, removable hard disk or on CD-ROM.

	Fast	Slow	Average
Text Only	0.08 hr/pg	0.45 hr/pg	0.18 hr/pg
	4.8 min/pg	27 min/pg	10.8 min/pg

FILM RECORDING

Convert computer files into 35mm negatives, does not include film processing.

	Fast	Slow	Average
4K Slide	0.2 minutes	12 minutes	2.32 minutes.

LASER SETTING

Convert computer file into paper or film output. Use your own machine standard.

	Fast	Slow	Average
Paper/Film	38 pg/min	2 pg/min	11.1 pg/min

IMAGESETTING

Convert computer file into RC paper or film output. Use your own machine standard.

	Fast	Slow	Average
RC Paper/Film	47.2 in/min	0.03 in/min	9.68 in/min

PHOTO CD MASTERING

Convert graphic images and photographs into computer data, save on CD-ROM. Use your own machine standard.

	Fast	Slow	Average
650 MB disc	40 minutes	38 minutes	39 minutes

CD-ROM ARCHIVING

Save computer data on CD-ROM. Use your own machine standard.

	Fast	Slow	Average
Small File	12 sec/file	17 sec/file	13.4 sec/file
Database File	50 sec/file	68 sec/file	58.8 sec/file
Large File	68 sec/file	80 sec/file	74.4 sec/file
Multisession Photo-CD	62 sec/file	88 sec/file	71.6 sec/file

Web Services

WEB SITE DESIGN

Create a concept, design each page and develop an image map for a site consisting of a splash page and multiple linked pages.

Simple	Complex	Average	Typical
5 hours	15 hours	12 hours	10 hours

WEB PAGE LAYOUT

Convert text, graphic images and photographs into HTML, CGI, GIF, JPG, etc., save on disk, and FTP upload files to client's site.

Simple	Complex	Average	Typical
1.23 hr/pg	3.14 hrs/pg	2.08 hrs/pg	1.6 hrs/pg
74 min/pg	188 min/pg	125 min/pg	96 min/pg

ADDITIONAL WEB PAGE

Simple	Complex	Average	Typical
0.5 hr/pg	0.9 hrs/pg	0.75 hrs/pg	1.85 hrs/pg
75 min/pg	185 min/pg	125 min/pg	111 min/pg

AUDIO (Add Clip to Site)

Simple	Complex	Average	Typical
0.29 hr/clip	0.57 hr/clip	0.43 hr/clip	0.40 hr/clip
17.4 min/clip	34.2 min/clip	25.8 min/clip	24 min/clip

AUDIO (Record & Edit)

Simple	Complex	Average	Typical
0.6 hr/clip	0.77 hr/clip	0.69 hr/clip	0.7 hr/clip
36 min/clip	46 min/clip	41 min/clip	42 min/clip

BACKGROUND (Add Background)

Simple	Complex	Average	Typical
0.4 hr/pg	1.2 hrs/pg	0.68 hrs/pg	0.5 hrs/pg
24 min/pg	72 min/pg	41 min/pg	30 min/pg

BANNER (Basic)

Simple	Complex	Average	Typical
0.6 hr/each	2.5 hrs/each	1.42 hrs/each	1.2 hrs/each
36 min/each	150 min/each	85.2 min/each	72 min/each

BANNER (Animated)

Simple	Complex	Average	Typical
0.8 hr/each	2.6 hrs/each	1.5 hrs/each	1.25 hrs/each
48 min/each	156 min/each	90 min/each	75 min/each

CONTENT DEVELOPMENT

Simple	Complex	Average	Typical
0.75 hr/pg	1.0 hrs/pg	0.75 hrs/pg	0.75 hrs/pg
45 min/pg	60 min/pg	45 min/pg	45 min/pg

VIDEO (Add Clip to Site)

Simple	Complex	Average	Typical
0.41 hr/clip	4.3 hr/clip	3.02 hr/clip	3.8 hr/clip
25 min/clip	258 min/clip	181.2 min/clip	228 min/clip

FORM DESIGN (Basic)

Simple	Complex	Average	Typical
0.67 hr/form	1.2 hr/form	.9 hr/form	0.8 hr/form
40.2 min/form	72 min/form	54 min/form	48 min/form

FORM DESIGN (Interactive)

Simple	Complex	Average	Typical
0.56 hr/each	1.6 hr/each	1.0 hr/each	0.6 hr/each
33.6 min/each	108 min/each	60 min/each	36 min/each

HIT COUNTER

Simple	Complex	Average	Typical
0.2 hr/each	0.2 hrs/each	0.2 hrs/each	0.2 hrs/each
12 min/each	12 min/each	12 min/each	12 min/each

IMAGE MAPS

Simple	Complex	Average	Typical
0.57 hr/map	0..83 hrs/map	0.7 hrs/map	0.7 hrs/map
34.2 min/map	49.8 min/map	42 min/map	42 min/map

LINKING

Simple	Complex	Average	Typical
0.08 hr/link	0.28 hrs/link	0.14 hrs/link	0.12 hrs/link
5 min/link	16.8 min/link	9 min/link	7.2 min/link

PROGRAMMING (Java)

Simple	Complex	Average	Typical
0.33 hr/pg	0.67 hrs/pg	0.56 hrs/pg	0.5 hrs/pg
19.8 min/pg	40.2 min/pg	33.6 min/pg	30 min/pg

SITE REDESIGN

Simple	Complex	Average	Typical
1 hr/pg	1 hrs/pg	1 hrs/pg	1 hrs/pg
60 min/pg	60 min/pg	60 min/pg	60 min/pg

PROOFREAD SITE

Simple	Complex	Average	Typical
0.4 hr/pg	0.5 hrs/pg	0.45 hrs/pg	0.4 hrs/pg
24 min/pg	30 min/pg	27 min/pg	24 min/pg

FRAMES

Simple	Complex	Average	Typical
1 hr/each	2 hrs/each	1.5 hrs/each	1.5 hrs/eac
60 min/each	120 min/each	90 min/each	90 min/each

GUEST BOOK

Simple	Complex	Average	Typical
1.3 hr/each	1.4 hrs/each	1.33 hrs/each	1.3 hrs/each
78 min/each	84 min/each	80 min/each	78 min/each

MESSAGE BOARD

Simple	Complex	Average	Typical
2.6 hr/ea	2.7 hrs/ea	2.67 hrs/ea	2.67 hrs/ea
156 min/ea	162 min/ea	160 min/ea	160 min/ea

NON JAVA CHAT ROOM

Simple	Complex	Average	Typical
2 hr/ea	2 hrs/ea	2.0 hrs/ea	2.0 hrs/ea
120 min/ea	120 min/ea	120 min/ea	120 min/ea

Other Production Times

3D ANIMATION

Produce 350K AVI	1.07 hr/finished sec

AUDIO CD-ROM

Transfer Audio DA to CD-WO	3 hrs/disc
Direct audio to DAT	3 hours

BOOK EVALUATION

Review manuscript before layout	4.8 hrs/evaluation

BOOK INDEXING

Index complete book text body	0.12 hr/pg

CUSTOM WEB GIF/ANIMATION

Design from scratch	3.3 hr each

DIGITAL PHOTOGRAPHY

65 images for monthly newspaper insert	4 days

RESEARCH

on-line research	21 min/pg

TV NEWS SPOT

30 second ad for television	10 hrs/30 sec ad

VIDEO ARCHIVING (MPEG Encoding)

$10,000/1 hour tape @ $125/hr	80 hrs/60 min tape

Custom Operator Standards

The concept is simple. The implementation is time-intensive. Custom production times help you quickly generate a general idea how long a particular job may take. By knowing the time to do specific tasks and by knowing the jobs already scheduled, you can provide your customer a pretty good idea when their job will be ready.

The trick is to determine what to measure and how many measurements to take. Start by partitioning the operations in your shop into cost categories (e.g., keyboarding, layout and design, graphics, typesetting, prepress, bindery, etc.) The National Association of Printers and Lithographers (NAPL) identified 13 different production areas in desktop service—six single color functions and seven process color functions. These include keyboarding, scanning, page composition, proofreading, black and white or color proofing, final output, and final proofs.

Make your own list of those production functions that you perform and construct a model that generates time metrics for each. I've selected several production models that you can adopt and use to produce custom timing standards. The first involves a project-task logging sheet to record timing information for every function performed in your shop. The second is more detailed and involves special task logging sheets that break functions and tasks into specific actions that are measureable. Each of these will be discussed in this section.

Operator Performance Timing Model 1

In this model you generate a historical log of how long it takes each person to perform billable work. Since both time and costs are critical in pricing, you can develop an Activity Time Worksheet for each job and task. On this form you can estimate the time spent on indirect project activities. Develop shorthand codes for each function. Then start collecting timing information. Be aware that measuring time to perform requires discipline and habit. Ask each person to log the time that they spend performing various tasks. This will take about 10 minutes a day—an acceptable investment in time to get useful data. Follow-up to be certain that times are actually being recorded.

On the next page is a time tracking form that you could adopt for your business.

Activity Time Tracking Form

Date _______________   Employee _________________________

Project	Task	Time In	Time Out	Total Time

This form is ideally suited for your spreadsheet. All you need is five columns, one formula to determine the total time, and another formula to calculate average time for each function. By using a 24-hour time format (e.g., 0800 for 8:00 a.m., 1200 for noon, 2400 for midnight), your computer can easily subtract the time out from the time in to get total time expended on each task. Then it can add all the total times for a specific task and divide the result by the number of times the task was performed to generate an average time per task.

The times listed for each task will vary based on job complexity, equipment used and individual involved. Not only will one person take less time to perform the same task than another, but you yourself will take more time one day to de a task than you will on another day. This is a reality when people are involved in the process. The goal is to find the average time for performing each task at several levels of complexity.

As you collect time-motion data, don't reveal the individual time results to others on your staff. Keep this to yourself and the orginator of the data. Show by example that you use time-function information to assign workers to their best tasks. And show by example that you also use the information to plan training and skill sessions.

If you intend to apply pay for performance, understand that if you tell employees that they'll be paid based on their productivity, most will focus on the easy jobs to keep their productivity figure high. The detail to which you partition jobs into functional tasks will help keep the evaluation even. Just be certain to consider ALL work associated with a task. Productivity should include direct labor and the rework resulting from pushing so hard that errors occur. Corrections can take as long as doing it right the first time.

After tracking time-to-perform over a period such as a month, a pattern will develop that shows the best, worst, and most likely times that each direct labor employee will take to complete specific functional tasks.

Operator Performance Timing Model 2

A better model is to generate a data collection form for each function similar to what you did for your machine standards. Model 2 takes a closer look at production time and gives you another unique way to collect timing information.

The worksheets that you use help you determine time based on measurement criteria (discussed earlier). For example, what information should you collect to generate a benchmark for keyboarding? What measurement criteria should you use? Most people select 1,000 characters and a set time period as their yardstick. Therefore, you want to determine how long it takes an average typist to keyboard 1,000 characters. Do the same for each function that is performed in producing billable work.

On your worksheet, specify the various types of work (e.g., simple, standard, complex). Assume that the hardware and software are ready for operation. Then list the start and stop times for each function on each project. The start time does not include set-up time. A separate time worksheet will be used for each task on a project. Therefore, you could have five time worksheets associated with a single project.

Each time you do a job, generate detailed worksheets on the functional activities. A range of times-per-task will develop. From these you can determine the average time it takes to perform. Assuming that you are at least as motivated as the most productive person in your shop, you can use your results to compare with those of the other workers.

On the following pages are formats that you can adopt for developing an operator production standard for various functions performed in your shop. The first covers keyboarding.

Example - Keyboarding

System Configuration: Computer: _486DX, 100 MHz, 16 MB RAM, 520 MB HD_
Software Application Used: _Word 6.0_

Project Task	Time Start	Time End	Difficulty Low	Difficulty Moderate	Difficulty High	# Words	# Char	# Pages	Char per page	Total minutes	Char per min
manual	1030	1130		√		1390	10800	6.25	1,728	60	180
booklet	0900	1100	√			5250	31500	5	1050	120	350
report	14								1719	150	126
book interior	07.								800	240	70
brochure	13								2680	90	60
manual	09..								1500	180	225
TV script	0700	1200		√		3600	23400	39	600	120	195

Difficulty of Task	Number Jobs	Total Characters/Minute	Average Characters/Minute
Low	2	575	287.5
Moderate	3	435	145.0
High	2	196	98.0

Keyboarding

System Configuration: Computer: _______________________________

Software Application Used: _______________________

Project Task	Time Start	Time End	Difficulty Low	Moderate	High	# Words	# Char	# Pages	Char per page	Total minutes	Char per min
____	____	____	____	____	____	____	____	____	____	____	____
____	____	____	____	____	____	____	____	____	____	____	____
____	____	____	____	____	____	____	____	____	____	____	____
____	____	____	____	____	____	____	____	____	____	____	____
____	____	____	____	____	____	____	____	____	____	____	____
____	____	____	____	____	____	____	____	____	____	____	____
____	____	____	____	____	____	____	____	____	____	____	____

Difficulty of Task	Number Jobs	Total Characters/Minute	Average Characters/Minute
Low	________	________	________
Moderate	________	________	________
High	________	________	________

Use the software that came with this special report to generate a separate set of forms for each computer system used for keyboarding data. Look for the best, worst, and typical times based on the resources available. You can establish a baseline production model after collecting a number of sample points. The averages become your standard keyboarding times.

Likewise, an operator standard can be developed for page layout. In this case, develop a template for each size page—letter, legal, and tabloid—and for each complexity—text only, 30% art, and 70% art. On the following pages are sample forms that you can adopt to collect data on page layout, scan retouch, color editing and typography. Times do not include set-up. Assume the system is already setup and ready for each function.

Example
Page Layout (letter size)

Computer: *Macintosh Quadra 100 MHz, 16MB, 700 MB HS*
Software Application Used: *Pagemaker 6.0*
Project: *Product Manual*

Date (Start): *January 12, 1999*   (Finish): *January 13, 1999*

Page Number	Text Only	Complexity 30% Art	70% Art	Start Time	Stop Time	Total Time Expended (hrs/min)
1	√			0815	0916	1:01
2		√		0920	1040	1:20
3		√		1045	1215	1:30
4	√			1330	1435	1:05
5	√			1440	1540	1:00
6						0:55
7						0:54
8	√			0940	1039	0:59
9		√		1045:	1220	1:35
10			√	1330	1515	1:45
11			√	1530	1720	1:50
12						
13						
14						
15						

Difficulty	Total Pages	Total Time	Average Hours/Page
Text Only	6	5.54	0:59
30% Art	3	4:25	1:25
70% Art	2	3:35	1:47

Page Layout (letter size)

Computer: _______________________________________

Software Application Used: ____________________

Project: _________________________________

Date (Start): __________________ (Finish): ___________________

Page Number	Complexity			Start Time	Stop Time	Total Time Expended (hrs/min)
	Text Only	30% Art	70% Art			
1	_____	_____	_____	_______	_______	_______
2	_____	_____	_____	_______	_______	_______
3	_____	_____	_____	_______	_______	_______
4	_____	_____	_____	_______	_______	_______
5	_____	_____	_____	_______	_______	_______
6	_____	_____	_____	_______	_______	_______
7	_____	_____	_____	_______	_______	_______
8	_____	_____	_____	_______	_______	_______
9	_____	_____	_____	_______	_______	_______
10	_____	_____	_____	_______	_______	_______
11	_____	_____	_____	_______	_______	_______
12	_____	_____	_____	_______	_______	_______
13	_____	_____	_____	_______	_______	_______
14	_____	_____	_____	_______	_______	_______
15	_____	_____	_____	_______	_______	_______

Difficulty	Total Pages	Total Time	Average Hours/Page
Text Only	_________	_________	______________
30% Art	_________	_________	______________
70% Art	_________	_________	______________

Page Layout (legal size)

Computer: ____

Software Application Used: _______________________________

Project: _______________________________________

Date (Start): _____________________ (Finish): _____________________

Page Number	Complexity			Start Time	Stop Time	Total Time Expended (hrs/min)
	Text Only	30% Art	70% Art			
1	_____	_____	_____	_____	_____	_____
2	_____	_____	_____	_____	_____	_____
3	_____	_____	_____	_____	_____	_____
4	_____	_____	_____	_____	_____	_____
5	_____	_____	_____	_____	_____	_____
6	_____	_____	_____	_____	_____	_____
7	_____	_____	_____	_____	_____	_____
8	_____	_____	_____	_____	_____	_____
9	_____	_____	_____	_____	_____	_____
10	_____	_____	_____	_____	_____	_____
11	_____	_____	_____	_____	_____	_____
12	_____	_____	_____	_____	_____	_____
13	_____	_____	_____	_____	_____	_____
14	_____	_____	_____	_____	_____	_____
15	_____	_____	_____	_____	_____	_____

Difficulty	Total Pages	Total Time	Average Hours/Page
Text Only	_______	_______	_______
30% Art	_______	_______	_______
70% Art	_______	_______	_______

Page Layout (tabloid size)

Computer: ____

Software Application Used: ___________________

Project: _______________________________

Date (Start): _________________ (Finish): _________________

Page Number	Complexity			Start Time	Stop Time	Total Time Expended (hrs/min)
	Text Only	30% Art	70% Art			
1	_____	_____	_____	_____	_____	_____
2	_____	_____	_____	_____	_____	_____
3	_____	_____	_____	_____	_____	_____
4	_____	_____	_____	_____	_____	_____
5	_____	_____	_____	_____	_____	_____
6	_____	_____	_____	_____	_____	_____
7	_____	_____	_____	_____	_____	_____
8	_____	_____	_____	_____	_____	_____
9	_____	_____	_____	_____	_____	_____
10	_____	_____	_____	_____	_____	_____
11	_____	_____	_____	_____	_____	_____
12	_____	_____	_____	_____	_____	_____
13	_____	_____	_____	_____	_____	_____
14	_____	_____	_____	_____	_____	_____
15	_____	_____	_____	_____	_____	_____

Difficulty	Total Pages	Total Time	Average Hours/Page
Text Only	_________	_________	_____________
30% Art	_________	_________	_____________
70% Art	_________	_________	_____________

Typography

Date: _________________   Project: _________________________________

Computer: ____

Software: _____________________________________   Initial Page Count: _____

Form of How Work Was Submitted: _______________________   Final Page Count: _____

Page #	Time Start	Time End	Typefaces or Fonts Used	# Point Sizes	# Char	# Words	Total Time	Pages per Hour	Characters per Hour

Total Pages Typeset	Average Pages/Hour	Average Hours/Page

Scan Retouch

Date: _________________ Project: ___________________________

Computer: ____

Retouch Software Used: _____________________

File Type: ___________ File Size: ___________

Scan Size: _______________ File Name: ___________________

Start-up/Set-up Time (minutes)	Simple	Complexity Average	Difficult	Start Time	Stop Time	Total Time Expended

Date: _________________ Project: ___________________________

Computer: ____

Retouch Software Used: _____________________

File Type: ___________ File Size: ___________

Scan Size: _______________ File Name: ___________________

Start-up/Set-up Time (minutes)	Simple	Complexity Average	Difficult	Start Time	Stop Time	Total Time Expended

Total Scans Retouched	Total Time	Average Minutes/Retouch
Simple		
Average		
Difficult		

Color Editing

Date: _________________ Project: _______________________

Computer: ____

Software: _________________ File Name: ___________________

File Type: __________ File Size: ___________

Start-up/Set-up Time (minutes)	Complexity			Start Time	Stop Time	Total Time
	Simple	Average	Difficult			

Date: _________________ Project: _______________________

Computer: ____

Software: _________________ File Name: ___________________

File Type: __________ File Size: ___________

Start-up/Set-up Time (minutes)	Complexity			Start Time	Stop Time	Total Time
	Simple	Average	Difficult			

	Total Images Edited (Number)	Total Time (minutes)	Average Time (minutes:seconds)
Simple			
Average			
Difficult			

Factors Affecting Performance Times

The best operator production standards are those that you develop yourself. But recognize that changes in hardware, software, or production procedures can significantly alter the time baselines. So can intangible factors such as worker emotion and attitude.

The following are tangible and intangible factors that affect how well your staff will perform their tasks.

Tangible	Intangible
hardware	training
software	trade experience
system configuration	emotional attitude
facility layout	enthusiasm for job
software compatibility	perceived value to business
system interoperability	physical dexterity
access to resources	physical capacity
lighting	biorhythm state
ergonomics	last performance review
noise	relationships
work privacy	home environment
interruptions	work environment
schedule	

Some of these things you can directly affect. Others you must deal with by situation. The key is to recognize that many factors can affect how well and how fast you perform. Try to optimize those that you can control. Recognize that we all have good and less good days. Seek the average production performance. And then keep on top of the "standard" operator production times that you develop.

As you upgrade your hardware and software, you'll find certain jobs take less time to perform. We upgraded our OCR scanning software and discovered that scanning and interpretation of text took less than half the original time. This translates directly into production cost benefits for you.

Number of Measurements to Take

For years, business psychologists have conducted time-moton studies on workers. The banking industry consistently evaluates how long it should take for its employees to perform certain tasks. These timing metrics are incorporated into analyses used to determine how many full time equivalent employees a particular center requires to perform all of its repetitive functions. Time measurements are taken over a relatively long period and then updated annually. The averages are used to establish a standard production time from which to evaluate each operator .

In the early 1970s, General Electric published a guide defining the number of cycles to observe when developing time standards. They based their guide on the cycle time in minutes of a particular task activity. Essentially, GE recommended the following number of measurments:

Cycle Time (minutes)	Number of Cycles to Measure
0.10	200
0.25	100
0.50	60
0.75	40
1	30
2	20
2.1 to 5	15
5.1 to 10	10
10.1 to 20	8
20.1 to 40	5
40.1 +	3

This suggests that you should take 10 to 15 measurements of the time to image same-size photos using a drum scanner with a cycle time of five minutes per inch when developing a machine time standard for that piece of equipment.

Based on the GE study, and other time-motion studies, I suggest that you consider using the criteria shown on the next page when taking your own time measurements.

Function Time (minutes)	Number of Samples
1	60
10	50
20	40
30	30
45	20
60	10
>60	5

A useful byproduct of a time study is the learning curve.

The Learning Curve

If a thousand computer graphic designers are selected at random and then tested for the time it takes them to perform a particular task, say design a flyer, the times that they take can be plotted producing a unique curve as shown below. This shape is called a *normal distribution* curve. The concept is that taking 1,000 of anything and comparing it against a variable factor will produce a normal distribution that can be measured and evaluated.

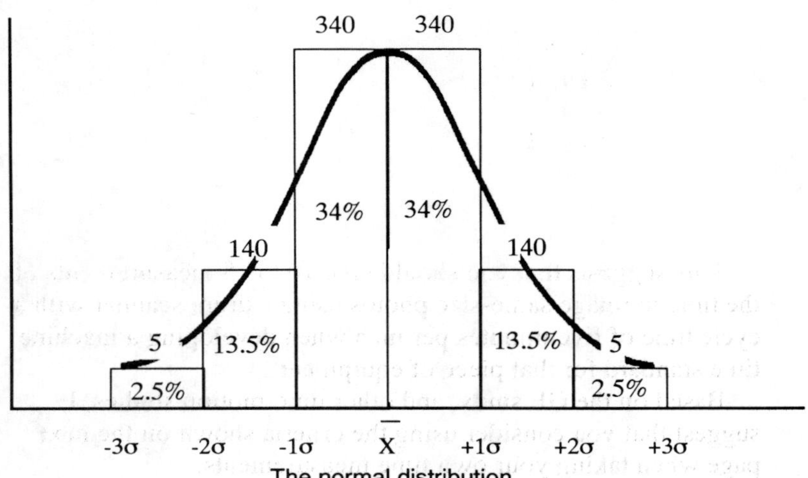

The normal distribution.

The center of the distribution curve is called the *normal,* the average, or X-bar. The amount of variation in the performance of individuals from this normal can be plotted from the slowest to the fastest. If enough samples are taken, a normal distribution curve results. This curve can be partitioned into variance values from the norm. Each variance distance is called a standard deviation or *"sigma"* (σ). It turns out that 68% of the samples (designers) will be within 1σ on either side of the normal (340 + 340 = 680), Ninety-five percent of the samples fall within two standard deviations of the mean, and within 3σ of the mean, 99.7% of the sample data will fall (assuming a normal distribution, of course).

By measuring a group of designers with similar backgrounds, training and experience you can generate a normal curve that has both ends pulled in toward the center. The lower the training and experience of the worker, the wider the distribution curve. The stronger the training and experience, the narrower (sharper) the distribution curve. This distribution phenomenon is called the *"learning curve."*

Learning is time dependent. The first time that a designer performs a task, the process can take hours. But as that person gains experience and knowledge, the time to perform decreases (productivity increases).

In Benjamin Niebel's book *Motion and Time Study,* the author recommends a typical learning curve based on unit time and cumulative production as shown in the figure below.

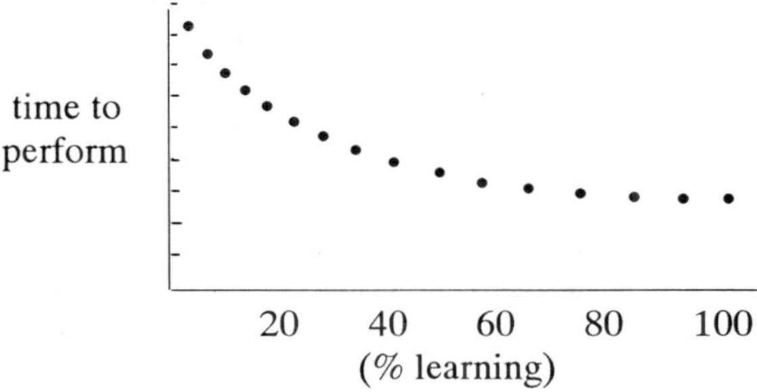

Many factors can affect this curve—a patient teacher, immediate and quality feedback, coaching and encouragement from the supervisor and rewards.

If you generate learning curves representing every major task in your shop, you can determine what is an acceptable standard of performance for each. Then you could use these standards as guides to identify the expected level of productivity that is characteristic of an average computer operator with a known degree of familiarity with each task.

Let's say that your shop designs 100 flyers each month. Fifty percent of these designs are single color simple text with about 30% graphics. You collect performance time data on producing 50 flyers in this category by the same person. By plotting the times, you are able to generate a learning curve on designing text/30% graphics flyers. The curve should approximate the figure shown on the previous page.

Then by plotting production time against cumulative flyers designed on a logarithmic (log-log) scale, you discover that the learning curve can be made to normalize to a straight line as shown below.

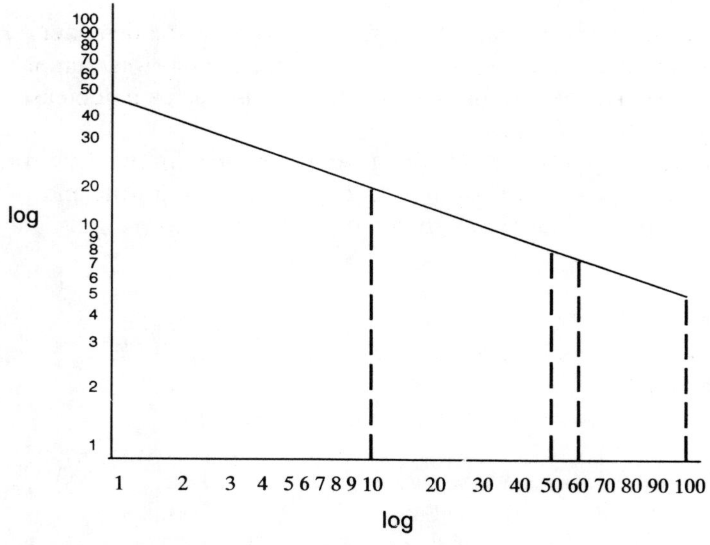

Having designed a flyer before has a pronounced effect on the point where the learning curve begins to flatten. Learning curve theory suggests that the per unit time will decline by some constant percentage as the total quantity of flyers designed doubles. If you expect an 80% improvement in design time, the average design time per flyer will decline by 20 percent with each doubling in the quantity produced. This is the affect of the log-log scale.

This learning curve percentage represents the slope of the log-log linear line. You can calculate the point on the learning curve percentage line with the following formula.

$$2^c = \frac{Tcum\ (set\ 2)}{Tcum\ (set\ 1)} = \frac{h[n(set\ 2)]^c}{h[n(set\ 1)]^c}$$

where

Tcum = total cumulative hours per unit for a set of units
h = labor hours to produce the first unit
n = number of complete units
c = slope of learning curve

Those of you with advanced math backgrounds will recall that multiplication can also be accomplished by converting the numbers to be multiplied into logarithms and then adding. Powers become multipliers in log equations. (A table of mathematical functions or math calculator is needed.)

Thus $Tcum - h[n]^c$ becomes

$$\log Tcum = \log h + c \log n$$

Slope c is calculated by dividing the log (percent of learning curve) by log base 2. This slope value is what you want because it lets you then find the learning curve percentage based on units produced (flyers designed).

For example, assume that you operate a logo design company. Your shop produces 50 logos at a cumulative average of 20 labor hours per logo. You want to determine the learning curve percentage after 100 logos are produced at a cumulative average of 15 labor hours per logo.

$n1$ = cumulative design to 50 unit point
$n2$ - cumulative design to 100 unit point

Applying each of these to the log Tca formula we get

$$\log Tca = \log h + c \log n$$

and for each cumulative average

$$\log 20 = \log h + c \, (\log 50)$$
$$\log 15 = \log h + c \, (\log 100)$$

a simultaneous equation. Then by subtracting one from the other,

$$\log 20 - \log 15 = \log h - \log h + c \, (\log 50) - c \, (\log 100)$$

and looking up the log values in a table, we get

$$(1.30103 - 1.17609) = c \, (1.69897 - 2.00000)$$

$$0.12494 = c \, (-0.30103)$$

$$c = \frac{0.12494}{-0.30103}$$

$$c = -0.415 \text{ (the slope is negative, tending downward)}$$

and

$$2^c = \text{learning curve}$$

Thus, by raising two to the power of c, the learning curve percentage can be calculated.

$$2^c = 2^{-0.415} = 75\%$$

On the next page is a handy table for converting slope to learning curve percentage.

Slope	Learning Curve Percentage
- 0.514	70
- 0.415	75
- 0.322	80
- 0.234	85
- 0.152	90
- 0.074	95

By monitoring the learning curve slope, you can deterine how fast your employees are coming up to speed on a particular service process or procedure. This is an excellent tool for recruiting and evaluating employees. And it is a mathematical way to use time studies to generate other useful data.

Develop Your Own Production Baseline

Combine your production time-study information with rules of thumb, historical records, and published industry standards to develop *baseline production standards* unique to your company.

As mentioned earlier, published industry standards are a helpful guide for comparison. Keep in mind, though, that your particular cost rates and production speeds may be higher or lower than published "standard" rates. That's why I call your own time rates baseline production standards. They incorporate outside metrics and guidelines with your own empirical measurements.

These resulting baseline standards are unique to your business. They represent the typical for your shop. Baseline production standards combine machine and personnel operating capabilities and compensate for differences between an industry standard and your particular shop. They're generated using all the information that you can collect. They not only establish standard performance times unique to your business (so you can quote flat rates on jobs), they are also useful for evaluating the performance of individual employees. Finally, baseline production standards are your best source for estimating project costs.

One helpful feature is that baseline standards establish all work at an average level. This means that efficient workers who finish faster and actually spend less time on a job don't cause a project to generate less revenue. Base your billing on standard operator times, not the actual performance times of individual workers. In this way, as your team gets more proficient, productivity increases and your profit margin grows.

If your custom standards are close to ours or other the standards of other organizations, you can realize a marketing advantage by advertising that your prices are based on "published industry standards." Many storefront shops display a statement near the front counter indicating the basis for their pricing. By basing rates on the average time to perform, you demonstrate that customers are consistently charged the same price for the same service. Here's an example of such a statement.

FOR YOUR PROTECTION

(Company Name) uses a common pricing system for desktop services based on industry production standards published by (name the source).

The basis for these standards is the average time required to perform specific duties related to project production by professional computer system operators.

As such, they protect you from being overcharged for work by a slower operator. Through consistent and equal task billing, all customers are charged the same price for the same service performed.

Sample production standard pricing statement.

Your baseline standards (incorporating machine and production standards) establish a time basis for each job in your shop. The machine standard says your printer can output eight sheets a minute. However, your system has a print spooler and multitasking capability. Thus you can command the computer to print this job in the background while you work on another job in the foreground.

Rather than charging each job for a portion of the time to warm-up, checkout, and execute the layout print actions, you bill out each job at the baseline standard full production rate. It's important to present consistent pricing to your customers.

Consider this case. A computer operator has several jobs to perform. After the first job is designed and page layout is complete, the operator commands a print output. Printing takes about 20 minutes, so while the printer is chugging out the first job, the operator begins work on the next job. This time-leveraging lets one person perform several tasks simultaneously. Yet you bill each job as if each were unique and had a dedicated person attending to the job during the full time of performance. This provides a cushion for rework caused by inadvertent errors or system breakdown.

Baseline production standards enable flat rate pricing, and more important, they prevent improvements in efficiency from reducing income by completing projects faster. Let's say that at some point, you decide to upgrade your hardware and software. You had been charging $40 an hour based on your cost using the old system configuration. When you install and place the new system into operation, you recalculate your costs basis and determine that you must now charge $55 an hour. This looks good until you realize that now you can perform the same job in half the time. Should the customer be charged only $67.50 for a job that previously they were paying you $90 to do?

You raised your rates, but face a possibility of bringing in less income for the same job. If you charge by the hour, rather than by the job, you could pass a production efficiency to your customer and earn less in the process. Owning the best equipment and current software is good, but shop owners tend to pass the time savings on to their clients. Pricing by the job can be better in several ways. You can keep your income stream high, yet when competition appears, you can bid a lower price—making you more competitive. You can also handle more jobs each work day.

As another example, you get an order to print camera ready copy of a 20-page catalog. You have several different computers and printers available for the job. Each machine operates at a different speed so the actual time to perform depends on the configuration that you use. The actual production time using the slower equipment can be much longer than the time to do the job with the newest and fastest hardware. If you base your estimate on production standards alone, you'll end up with two different prices for the same job.

Therefore, choose the longer time basis for your estimate to ensure that you cover costs and earn a profit regardless which machine configuration you use. The risk here is that your equipment may be so old that basing your bid on its slowest performance time could put your estimates outside the ballpark of customer acceptance. A competitor with new hardware and current software could out-produce and under-bid you.

Watch your use of historical information in timing jobs. History doesn't always repeat itself. Be careful that production inefficiencies aren't reflected in old time data. You may have developed your old standards using slower equipment and slower operators. You could have collected your historical data using a very skilled employee. Whenever you consider historical job-time data, clearly understand how it was developed. It helps if you convert historical data into baseline standards by extrapolating older machine capabilities to current configurations and comparing your task performance times with published production information. Keep current on evolving industry production standards since they will reflect new technologies and refined operating efficiencies.

By maintaining historical baseline standards you can identify trends and monitor shop efficiency and productivity based on actual averages custom to your business.

IV. Budgeted Hourly Rates

The key to flat rate pricing is the budgeted hourly rate. A unique BHR exists for each billable service that your shop provides. This section shows you how to develop custom BHR costs so you know how much you will earn or can negotiate away on every job that you do.

The budgeted hourly rates shown in this section are based on our survey. They are for comparison only. You should develop budgeted hourly rates that are custom to your own shop and use your own BHRs in generating flat rate prices to quote.

By multiplying each function's baseline production time by its budgeted hourly cost, you can calculate a budgeted cost for each task in a job. Then, by adding up the budgeted hourly costs for each activity, and adding material costs such as film and special paper, you can calculate a project cost to which profit, return on investment, and intangibles such as job turn-around time, design skill, and competitive advantage are added to achieve a final selling price. Partitioning any project into functional tasks and applying budgeted hourly rates to each task lets you bid a flat rate for any job.

You start by partitioning all of your shop's services into individual operations. For example, producing a newsletter could involve receiving text on a disk and converting the file into a usable form (file conversion), correcting typographical or grammar mistakes in the text (editing), designing a style sheet (design), importing graphics and text into an electronic page (layout), and generating a laser printout (print out). Each of these operations can have an associated budgeted hourly rate.

Once all of your operations are identified — keyboarding, file conversion, typography, scanning,, design, layout, print output, and so on—you specify the labor skills and equipment required for each operation. Consider every resource in your business — people, equipment, software, facility, and investment capital.

Then identify the annual costs of these resources as allocated to each operation. These costs will be fixed or variable. Next, determine an hourly overhead cost for the shop.

Each operation or function can be considered a cost category to be budgeted. You determine the number of chargeable hours that each cost category generates. Then, divide the total annual costs for each function by an estimate of the annual billable hours for that operation to get its budgeted hourly cost rate. Using these, you can price a job based on the combination of the individual hourly rates for each operation.

The more detailed you make your cost breakdown, the easier it is to define tasks and build budgeted hourly rates. The idea is to have the total shop's operating costs partitioned into chargeable activities. Each function is analyzed and production times are established. These times are converted to costs that you budget or allocate to each task. A job will be comprised of several specific tasks. Each task activity has an associated cost category and a budgeted hourly cost rate.

Once you have your budgeted hourly cost rates, factor in productivity, return on investment, and markup on the materials to generate a "straw-man" price that you can quote. Then look at your marketplace and your competition to establish hourly billing rates for each functional activity. These are the rates that you publish on your counter price sheets or that you quote.

A recent International Prepress Association survey concluded that the best approach for pricing desktop services is to establish a budgeted hourly rate for each piece or group of equipment worked on. This allocates (budgets) pricing to the hardware and software used to perform a job. Good time assessments on each type of project can help you apply proper markup and establish good budgeted hourly prices.

As work proceeds, keep a list or record of the average times to perform each task. Use these to update your baseline production standard. Don't forget "system start-up" and "modified start-up" (re-start) times. Many shops call this *"set up"* time. They often charge a flat rate for setting a system up to perform a specific service. This is where many *"minimum charge"* prices come from.

Incorporate start-up and re-start in your final bill. It can take several minutes for your computer system to initialize, run an application program and open in the job that you will be working. The first effort on a job includes setup time. Once the job format is established, then each time that you go back to the job, you must re-start the system—boot up the application program and open the job that were working on. The total job time should incorporate these re-start actions.

With budgeted hourly cost rates, you can factor in productivity, return on investment, profit, expected sales, the marketplace and your competition to generate a price basis for each task. Then when you price a job, you can separate out the activities and quote a job by tasks with unique rates for each task.

It's important to understand that both fixed and variable costs are used in determining your budgeted hourly rate for a particular service or profit center. If you vary the number of hours each day that the service is provided or the profit center is active, fixed costs can have a major impact on the budgeted hourly rate that you calculate. Essentially this means that the more utilization you have, the lower the effect of fixed costs on your budgeted hourly rate because you spread the fixed costs out over more operational hours. Essentially the effect of overhead is spread out.

Likewise an under-utilized function or profit center can have a higher budgeted hourly rate (caused by a higher overhead). This can prevent your shop from being competitive in certain service areas.

Because it depends on industry or custom production standards, the budgeted hourly rate method can provide an easy way to quickly price a job. A shop's billing baseline depends on the type of job and the customer. Many new owner-operators initially apply a fixed hourly rate to every service (shop rate). With experience, some develop a unique hourly rate for each service that they provide. Then they fine tune these hourly rates and establish page, image, or word count baselines for pricing.

Budgeted Hourly Rate Example

Home Business

The following example shows how to calculate budgeted hourly rates for a small desktop publishing business. This hypothetical shop operates out of a home office and earns $70,000 a year in revenue. To make the example as basic as possible, assume this business has a single employee, the owner-operator. This owner-operator uses 20 percent of the home (about 200 square feet) strictly for the business.

The business has been operating for one year. The owner takes no vacation and works 2,080 hours a year (52 weeks, 40 hours a week). The sources of income for the business can be partitioned into:

Keyboarding	10%	$7,000
Scanning	10%	7,000
Creative Design	20%	14,000
Page Layout	50%	35,000
Laser Printing	10%	7,000
		======
		$70,000

To perform these functions, the owner purchased a computer, a laser printer and a scanner with word processing, scanning and page layout software. Total investment was $10,000 ($5,000 in purchases depreciated over five years and $5,000 written off this year).

The objective is to determine a budgeted hourly rate for each activity. This means identifying fixed and variable costs for labor and materials, and specifying and allocating a baseline production standard to each activity. Below are the fixed and variable costs associated with this business.

FIXED COSTS

Rent (Indirect/Overhead)	
200 sq/ft @ $2.50 per sq ft per month = $500/month	6,000
Basic Utilities (Indirect/Overhead) @ 20% of household costs	
Telephone - $25/month @ 20% (300/yr x 0.2 = $60/yr)	
Gas - $13/month @ 20% (156/yr x 0.2 = $31.20/yr)	
Electricity - $50/month @ 20% (600/yr x 0.2 = $120/yr)	
Water - $25/month @ 20% (300/yr x 0.2 = $60/yr)	272
Property Insurance (Indirect/Overhead)	
$1,200/yr @ 20% = $240/yr	240
Taxes (Indirect/Overhead) 11%	7,500
Depreciation (Indirect/Overhead) 20%/yr	1,000
Hardware Not Depreciated (Indirect) 100%	5,000
Software to Run Business (Indirect/Overhead)	500
Documentation to Operate Business (Indirect/Overhead)	100
Office Cleaning (Indirect/Overhead)	360
Grounds Keeping (Indirect/Overhead)	48
Vehicle Insurance (Indirect/Overhead)	1,200
Vehicle Purchase Loan (Indirect/Overhead)	4,800
	========
Total Annual Fixed Cost:	$31,080

VARIABLE COSTS

Marketing Expenses (Indirect/Overhead) 3%	$2,100
Advertising Expenses (Indirect/Overhead) 3%	2,100
Salaries — Owner-Operator (Indirect/Overhead)	21,840
Salaries — Owner-Operator Working on Jobs (Direct)	9,360
Wages - Part Time Help (Direct)	1,000
Cost of Goods Sold (Direct)	100
Supplies Used to Do Job (Direct)	100
Fringe Benefits (Indirect)	936
Vehicle Operation (Indirect)	500
	========
Total Variable Cost:	$38,036
TOTAL ANNUAL FIXED & VARIABLE COSTS	$68,116

Annual fixed and variable costs for a home desktop services business.

Notice in our example, that this home business made a profit of $1,884 on the $70,000 income—about three percent. Not bad, but the owner-operator is paying $6,000 in rent each year for using the owner-operator's own home. This is additional income (although taxable) to the home business owner.

You'd think that salaries should be a fixed cost. But many entrepreneurs defer paying a salary while building their business. And, later, if the work load decreases during economic declines, independent business owners usually reduce their own salaries first to keep things going—hence salaries are variable.

Based on this cost breakdown, let's calculate a budgeted hourly rate for each activity performed by this home desktop publishing business. The following are budgeted hourly cost analysis forms for various services.

The allocation of costs and assignment of productivity levels depends on the capabilities of your own shop. These forms are provided to give you an idea how to proceed. All numbers are rounded up to the nearest dollar. Similar blank worksheets are provided on the disk that accompanied this special report.

BUDGETED HOURLY RATES
Home Office
KEYBOARDING

INVESTMENT - Cost of computer system used: $2,500
INVESTMENT - Cost of software used: 375
SPACE needed to perform this function (square feet):   20
PEOPLE - Percent of time a person is involved in activity: 100%
HOURLY PAY - Typical pay for keyboarding is $7 an hour.
  Since this is a one-person business, both the pre-defined
  $15/hour and $7/hour rates are used for calculating a
  budgeted hourly rate.
ANNUAL HOURS each person works (40 hrs/wk, 52 wks)   2,080

FIXED (NON VARIABLE) COSTS	@ $15/hr	@ $7/hr
Space Rent ($1.00/sq ft, 20 sq ft)	240	240
Depreciation (computer sys, 5 yrs @ 20% per year)	500	500
System Insurance ($4/M of investment)	8	8
Basic Utilities (20%)	27	27
Other fixed costs ($)	10	10
TOTAL FIXED COSTS	785	785

VARIABLE COSTS	@ $15/hr	@ $7/hr
Wages - Direct Labor (@ 2,080 hrs/yr)	31,200	14,560
Pension Fund (@ 2% of labor)	624	291
Employee Health/Medical insurance (@$131/month)	1,572	1,572
Payroll Taxes (@11.35% of labor costs)*	3,541	1,653
Workers Comp Insurance		
($3/M of labor costs = 0.3%of labor costs)	94	44
Task-Related added utility costs	3	3
Direct Supplies (take as 1% of fixed and wage costs)	320	153
Repairs & Maintenance (@2% of hardware costs)	50	50
Software upgrades (@10% of investment)	38	38
Other variable costs	25	25
TOTAL VARIABLE COSTS	37,467	18,389
OTHER COSTS		
Other Misc. Costs (@10% fixed & variable costs)	3,825	1,917
SG&E (overhead = 20%)	7,650	3,835
TOTAL OTHER COSTS	11,475	5,752
TOTAL ALL COSTS	$49,727	$24,926
TOTAL HOURLY COSTS	$23.91	$11.98
BUDGETED COST/HOUR		
50% Productive	47.81	23.96
30% Productive	79.69	39.93

UNIT OF WORK OUTPUT PER HOUR:
50 wpm, 250 char/minute, 15,000 char/hr,
1500 char/pg ==> 10 pages/hr

COST PER 1000 CHARACTERS	@ $15/hr	@ $7/hr
50% Productive	3.19/M	1.60/M
30% Productive	5.31/M	2.66/M

COST PER PAGE	@ $15/hr	@ $7/hr
50% Productive	$4.78/pg	$2.40/pg
30% Productive	$7.97/pg	$3.99/pg

*(NOTE: Payroll taxes were recently raised to 12.4 percent.)

Budgeted hourly rates for keyboarding.

Notice in the table that wages are placed under the Variable Cost category (even though they come under Fixed Cost from an annual budget perspective). This is because various employees (with different hourly pay rates) can be assigned to do this task. It really doesn't matter in the end because both fixed and variable costs are included in the final BHR values.

The "Other Misc Cost" value in the table is sometimes called a *"margin of safety"* or *MOS*. This cushion is used to compensate for costs that were forgotten in the budget, or to cover unforeseen events and conditions. It's an arbitrary value. In the calculations, I used 10 percent of the fixed and variable costs for the number to plug into the calculation. Some owners use 10 percent of revenue as the MOS. It's in the budget because experienced operators know that you'll always need "just a little more" the next time you calculate budgeted hourly costs.

To these budgeted prices you add profit and return on any initial investment to start the company. This gives you a reference price. Then set the actual price at what the market will bear.

BUDGETED HOURLY RATES
Home Office
SCANNING

INVESTMENT - Cost of computer and scanner system used: $5,000
INVESTMENT: Cost of software used: 375
SPACE needed to perform this function (square feet): 20
PEOPLE - Percent of time a person is involved in activity: 100%
HOURLY PAY: Owner's $15/hour and typical $8/hour
ANNUAL HOURS each person (40 hrs/wk, 52 wks) 2,080

FIXED (NON VARIABLE) COSTS	@ $15/hr	@ $8/hr
Space Rent ($1.00/sq ft, 20 sq ft)	240	240
Depreciation (5 yrs @ 20% per year)	1,000	1,000
System Insurance ($4/M of investment)	40	40
Basic Utilities (20%)	27	27
Other fixed costs ($)	10	10
TOTAL FIXED COSTS	1,317	1,317

VARIABLE COSTS	@ $15/hr	@ $8/hr
Wages - Direct Labor (@ 2,080 hrs/yr)	31,200	16,640
Pension Fund (@ 2% of labor)	624	333

Employee Health/Medical insurance | 1,572 | 1,572
Payroll Taxes (@11.35% of labor costs) | 3,541 | 1,889
Workers Comp Insurance (0.3%of labor costs) | 94 | 50
Task-Related added utility costs | 3 | 3
Direct Supplies (taken as 1% of fixed and wage costs) 325 | 180
Repairs & Maintenance (@2% of hardware costs) | 50 | 50
Software upgrades (@10% of investment) | 38 | 38
Other variable costs | 25 | 25
  TOTAL VARIABLE COSTS | 37,472 | 20,780

OTHER COSTS
Other Misc. Costs (@10% fixed & variable costs) | 3,879 | 2,210
SG&E Costs (overhead = 20%) | 7,758 | 4,419
  TOTAL OTHER COSTS | 11,637 | 6,629

  TOTAL ALL COSTS | $50,426 | $28,726
  TOTAL HOURLY COSTS | 24.24/hr | 13.81/hr
COST/HOUR
  50% Productive | $48.49/hr | $27.62/hr
  30% Productive | $80.81/hr | $46.04/hr

UNIT OF WORK OUTPUT PER HOUR:
Line Art ==> 4.92 scans/hr (includes minor cleanup and saving on disk)

COST PER SCAN - LINE ART | @ $15/hr | @ $8/hr
  50% Productive | $9.86/scan | $5.61/scan
  30% Productive | $16.42/scan | $9.36/scan

BUDGETED HOURLY RATES
Home Office
CREATIVE DESIGN

PEOPLE - Percent of time a person is involved in activity: | 100%
INVESTMENT - Cost of computer system used | $2,500
INVESTMENT - Cost of software used | 500
SPACE needed to perform this function (square feet) | 20
PEOPLE - Percent of time a person is involved in activity | 100%
HOURLY PAY | $15/hour
ANNUAL HOURS each person works (40 hrs/wk, 52 wks) | 2,080

FIXED (NON VARIABLE) COSTS	@ $15/hr
Space Rent ($1.00/sq ft, 20 sq ft)	240
Depreciation (computer system, 5 yrs @ 20% per year)	500
System Insurance ($4/M of investment)	40
Basic Utilities (20%)	27
Other fixed costs ($)	10
TOTAL FIXED COSTS	817

VARIABLE COSTS	@ $15/hr
Wages - Direct Labor ($15/hr @ 2,080 hrs/yr)	31,200
Pension Fund (@ 2% of labor)	624
Employee Health/Medical insurance (@$131/month)	1,572
Payroll Taxes (@11.35% of labor costs)	3,541
Workers Comp Insurance ($3/M of labor costs)	94
Task-Related added utility costs	3
Direct Supplies (taken as 1% of fixed costs and wage costs)	320
Repairs & Maintenance (@2% of hardware costs)	50
Software upgrades (@10% of investment)	50
Other variable costs	25
TOTAL VARIABLE COSTS	37,479

OTHER COSTS	
Other Misc. Costs (@10% fixed & variable costs)	3,830
Sales, General & Administrative Costs (overhead = 20%)	7,659
TOTAL OTHER COSTS	11,489

TOTAL ALL COSTS	$49,785
TOTAL HOURLY COSTS	23.94/hr

COST/HOUR	
50% Productive	47.87/hr
30% Productive	79.78/hr

UNIT OF WORK OUTPUT PER HOUR:
Depends on creativity level of designer. Assume one page per hour.

COST PER DESIGN	
50% Productive	$47.87/design
30% Productive	79.78/design

BUDGETED HOURLY RATES
Home Office
PAGE LAYOUT

INVESTMENT - Cost of computer system used	$2,500
INVESTMENT - Cost of software used	500
SPACE needed to perform this function (square feet)	20
PEOPLE - Percent of time a person is involved in activity	100%
HOURLY PAY	$15/hour
ANNUAL HOURS each person works (40 hrs/wk, 52 wks)	2,080

FIXED (NON VARIABLE) COSTS	@ $15/hr
Space Rent ($1.00/sq ft, 20 sq ft)	240
Depreciation (computer system, 5 yrs @ 20% per year)	500
System Insurance ($4/M of investment)	40
Basic Utilities (20%)	27
Other fixed costs ($)	10
TOTAL FIXED COSTS	817

VARIABLE COSTS	@ $15/hr
Wages - Direct Labor ($15/hr @ 2,080 hrs/yr)	31,200
Pension Fund (@ 2% of labor)	624
Employee Health/Medical insurance (@$131/month)	1,572
Payroll Taxes (@11.35% of labor costs)	3,541
Workers Comp Insurance (0.3%of labor costs)	94
Task-Related added utility costs	3
Direct Supplies (taken as 1% of fixed costs and wage costs)	320
Repairs & Maintenance (@2% of hardware costs)	50
Software upgrades (@10% of investment)	50
Other variable costs	25
TOTAL VARIABLE COSTS	37,479

OTHER COSTS	
Other Misc. Costs (@10% fixed & variable costs)	3,830
Sales, General & Administrative Costs (overhead = 20%)	7,659
TOTAL OTHER COSTS	11,489

TOTAL ALL COSTS	$49,785
TOTAL HOURLY COSTS	23.94/hr
COST/HOUR	
50% Productive	47.87/hr
30% Productive	79.78/hr

UNIT OF WORK OUTPUT PER HOUR:
Newsletter: 1.34 hours/page

COST PER PAGE (NEWSLETTER)
   50% Productive $64.15/pg
   30% Productive   106.91/pg

BUDGETED HOURLY RATES
Home Office
LASER PRINTING

INVESTMENT - Cost of computer and laser printer:	$5,000
INVESTMENT: Cost of software used:	0
SPACE needed to perform this function (square feet):	20
PEOPLE - Percent of time a person is involved in activity:	20%
HOURLY PAY: Owner's $15/hour and typical $7/hour.	
ANNUAL HOURS each person works (40 hrs/wk, 52 wks)	2,080

FIXED (NON VARIABLE) COSTS	@ $15/hr	@ $8/hr
Space Rent ($1.00/sq ft, 20 sq ft)	240	240
Depreciation (5 yrs @ 20% per year)	1,000	1,000
System Insurance ($4/M of investment)	40	40
Basic Utilities (20%)	27	27
Other fixed costs ($)	10	10
TOTAL FIXED COSTS	1,317	1,317

VARIABLE COSTS	@ $15/hr	@ $8/hr
Wages - Direct Labor (@ 20% of 2,080 hrs/yr)	6,240	3,328
Pension Fund (@ 2% of labor)	125	67
Employee Health/Medical insurance (@$131/month)	1,572	1,572
Payroll Taxes (@11.35% of labor costs)	708	378
Workers Comp Insurance ($3/M of labor costs)	19	10
Task-Related added utility costs	3	3
Direct Supplies (taken as 1% of fixed and wage costs)	76	46
Repairs & Maintenance (@2% of hardware costs)	50	50
Software upgrades (@10% of investment)	0	0
Other variable costs	25	25
TOTAL VARIABLE COSTS	8,818	5,479

OTHER COSTS		
Other Misc. Costs (@10% fixed & variable costs)	1,014	680
SG&A (overhead = 20%)	2.027	1,359
TOTAL OTHER COSTS	3,041	2,039

	@ $15/hr	@ $8/hr
TOTAL ALL COSTS	$13,176	$8,835
TOTAL HOURLY COSTS	31.67/hr	21.24/hr

COST/HOUR
    50% Productive $48.49/hr $42.48/hr
    30% Productive $80.81/hr $70.79/hr

UNIT OF WORK OUTPUT PER HOUR:
6 pages/minute, 360 pages/hour

COST PER PAGE	@ $15/hr	@ $7/hr
50% Productive	$0.13/pg	$0.12/pg
30% Productive	$0.22/pg	$0.20/pg

Perhaps this is why laser printer output prices are coming down to around 10¢ a page. The next section deals with the same activities. But this time, the operations are performed by an entrepreneur working out of a storefront.

Budgeted Hourly Rate Example
Store Front

In this scenario, the same business is assumed, but it operates out of a 400 square foot storefront office with two employees. The first is the owner-operator, who takes $15.60 an hour. The second is a computer operator—paid $7.28 an hour. This hypothetical shop earns $150,000 a year in revenue.

The business has been operating for one year. Both of the employees take one week vacation and get paid for five holidays when the shop is closed. The shop has 2,000 annual productive hours at 100%productivity (2,080 hours less 40 hours vacation less 40 hours holiday = 2,000 hours). The sources of income for the business can be partitioned into:

Keyboarding	10%	$15,000
Scanning	10%	15,000
Creative Design	20%	30,000
Page Layout	50%	75,000
Laser Printing	10%	15,000
		======
		$150,000

To operate the business, the owner purchased a computer, a laser printer and a scanner with word processing, scanning and page layout software. Total investment was $10,000 ($5,000 in purchases depreciated over five years and $5,000 in purchases written off this year).

The objective is to determine a budgeted hourly rate for each activity listed above just as we did for the home business.

The following example shows the fixed and variable costs associated with this storefront business.

FIXED COSTS

Rent (Indirect/Overhead)

400 sq/ft @ $2.50 per sq ft per month = $1,000/month	12,000

Basic Utilities (Indirect/Overhead) — 2,460
Insurance (Indirect/Overhead) — 1,200

Taxes (Indirect/Overhead)

Federal	28,500	
State	16,500	
Local	1,000	
Payroll	4,348	50,348

Depreciation (Indirect/Overhead) — 1,000
Hardware Not Depreciated (Indirect) — 5,000
Software to Run Business (Indirect/Overhead) — 500
Documentation to Operate Business (Indirect/Overhead) — 100
Office Cleaning (Indirect/Overhead) — 1,800
Grounds Keeping (Indirect/Overhead) — 960
Vehicle Insurance (Indirect/Overhead) — 1,200
Vehicle Purchase Loan (Indirect/Overhead) — 4,800

========

Total Fixed Cost: $81,368

VARIABLE COSTS

Marketing Expenses (Indirect/Overhead) — $4,500
Advertising Expenses (Indirect/Overhead) — 4,500
Salaries — Owner-Operator ($15.00/hr) — 31,200
Salaries — Computer Operator ($7.28/hr) — 14,560
Wages - Part Time Help (Direct) — 1,000
Cost of Goods Sold (Direct) — 100
Supplies Used to Do Job (Direct) — 1,000
Fringe Benefits (Indirect) — 1,372
Vehicle Operation (Indirect) — 500
New Software Required for Job (Direct) — 1,500
Documentation Purchased to Support Job (Direct) — 100

========

Total Variable Cost: $60,332

TOTAL FIXED & VARIABLE COSTS $141,700

Fixed and variable costs for storefront business.

Based on this cost breakdown, the following charts show how a budgeted hourly rate is calculated for each activity performed by this storefront desktop services business. As in the last example, figures are provided covering keyboarding, scanning, creative design, layout and laser printing.

BUDGETED HOURLY RATES
Storefront
KEYBOARDING

INVESTMENT - Cost of computer system used:	$2,500
INVESTMENT: Cost of software used:	375
SPACE needed to perform this function (square feet):	20
PEOPLE - Percent of time a person is involved in activity:	100%
HOURLY PAY- $7.28	
ANNUAL HOURS (40 hrs/wk, 50 wks, 2 wks sick/vacation)	2,000

FIXED (NON VARIABLE) COSTS	@ $7.28/hr
Space Rent ($2.50/sq ft, 20 sq ft = $50/mo = $600/yr)	600
Depreciation (computer system, 5 yrs @ 20% per year)	500
System Insurance ($4/M of investment)	8
Basic Utilities (20%)	27
Other fixed costs ($)	10
TOTAL FIXED COSTS	1,145

VARIABLE COSTS	@ $7.28/hr
Wages - Direct Labor ($7.28/hr @ 2,080 hrs/yr)	15,142
Wages - Indirect Labor (10% of supervision required)	1,514
Pension Fund (@ 2% of labor)	333
Employee Health/Medical insurance (@$131/month)	1,572
Payroll Taxes (@11.35% of labor costs)	1,891
Workers Comp Insurance ($3/M of labor costs = 0.3%of labor costs) 50	
Task-Related added utility costs	3
Direct Supplies (take as 1% of fixed costs and wage costs)	178
Repairs & Maintenance (@2% of hardware costs)	50
Software upgrades (@10% of investment)	38
Other variable costs	25
TOTAL VARIABLE COSTS	20,796

OTHER COSTS
Other Misc. Costs (@10% fixed & variable costs)   2,194
SG&A (overhead = 30% of fixed & variable)   6,582
   TOTAL OTHER COSTS   <u>8,776</u>

   TOTAL ALL COSTS $30,717
   TOTAL HOURLY COSTS (2,000 actual hours) $15.36/hr

BUDGETED COST/HOUR
   50% Productive   30.72
   30% Productive   51.20

UNIT OF WORK OUTPUT PER HOUR:
50 wpm, 250 char/minute, 15,000 char/hr,
1500 char/pg ==> 10 pages/hr

COST PER 1000 CHARACTERS
   50% Productive $2.05/M
   30% Productive $3.41/M

COST PER PAGE
   50% Productive $3.07/pg
   30% Productive $5.12/pg

Budgeted hourly rates for keyboarding.

BUDGETED HOURLY RATES
Storefront
SCANNING

INVESTMENT - Cost of computer and scanner system used $5,000
INVESTMENT: Cost of software used 375
SPACE needed to perform this function (square feet) 20
PEOPLE - Percent of time a person is involved in activity 100%
HOURLY PAY - $7.28/hour
ANNUAL HOURS (40 hrs/wk, 50 wks, 2 wks sick/vacation) 2,000

FIXED (NON VARIABLE) COSTS	@ $7.28/hr
Space Rent ($2.50/sq ft, 20 sq ft, $50/mo, $600/yr)	600
Depreciation (5 yrs @ 20% per year)	1,000
System Insurance ($4/M of investment)	20
Basic Utilities (20%)	27
Other fixed costs ($)	10
TOTAL FIXED COSTS	1,657

VARIABLE COSTS	@ $7.28/hr
Wages - Direct Labor ($7.28/hr @ 2,080 hrs/yr)	15,142
Wages - Indirect Labor (10% of supervision required)	1,514
Pension Fund (@ 2% of labor)	333
Employee Health/Medical insurance (@$131/month)	1,572
Payroll Taxes (@11.35% of labor costs)	1,891
Workers Comp Insurance ($3/M of labor costs)	50
Task-Related added utility costs	3
Direct Supplies (take as % of fixed costs and wage costs)	183
Repairs & Maintenance (@2% of hardware costs)	50
Software upgrades (@10% of investment)	38
Other variable costs	25
TOTAL VARIABLE COSTS	20,801

OTHER COSTS	
Other Misc. Costs (@10% fixed & variable costs)	2,246
SG&A Costs (overhead = 30% fixed & variable)	6,737
TOTAL OTHER COSTS	8,983

TOTAL ALL COSTS	$31,441
TOTAL HOURLY COSTS (2,000 actual hours)	$15.72/hr

COST/HOUR
    50% Productive $31.44/hr
    30% Productive $52.40/hr

UNIT OF WORK OUTPUT PER HOUR:
Line Art ==> 4.92 scans/hr (includes minor cleanup and saving on disk)

COST PER SCAN - LINE ART
    50% Productive $6.39/scan
    30% Productive $10.65/scan

Budgeted hourly rates for scanning line art.

BUDGETED HOURLY RATES
Storefront
CREATIVE DESIGN

INVESTMENT - Cost of computer system used	$2,500
INVESTMENT - Cost of software used	500
SPACE needed to perform this function (square feet)	20
PEOPLE - Percent of time a person is involved in activity	100%
HOURLY PAY - $15/hour	
ANNUAL HOURS (40 hrs/wk, 50 wks, 2 wks sick/vacation)	2,000

FIXED (NON VARIABLE) COSTS	@ $15/hr
Space Rent ($2.50/sq ft, 20 sq ft)	600
Depreciation (computer system, 5 yrs @ 20% per year)	500
System Insurance ($4/M of investment)	10
Basic Utilities (20%)	27
Other fixed costs ($)	10
TOTAL FIXED COSTS	1,147

VARIABLE COSTS	@ $15/hr
Wages - Direct Labor ($15/hr @ 2,080 hrs/yr)	31,200
Wages - Indirect Labor (10% of supervision required)	3,120
Pension Fund (@ 2% of labor)	686
Employee Health/Medical insurance (@$131/month)	1,572
Payroll Taxes (@11.35% of labor costs)	3,895
Workers Comp Insurance ($3/M of labor costs)	103
Task-Related added utility costs	3
Direct Supplies (taken as 1% of fixed costs and wage costs)	355
Repairs & Maintenance (@2% of hardware costs)	50
Software upgrades (@10% of investment)	50
Other variable costs	25
TOTAL VARIABLE COSTS	41,059

OTHER COSTS	
Other Misc. Costs (@10% fixed & variable costs)	4,221
Sales, General & Administrative Costs (overhead = 30% fixed & variable)	12,662
TOTAL OTHER COSTS	16,883

TOTAL ALL COSTS	$59,089
TOTAL HOURLY COSTS (2,000 actual hours)	$29.54/hr

COST/HOUR
50% Productive   59.09/hr
30% Productive   98.48/hr

UNIT OF WORK OUTPUT PER HOUR:
Depends on creativity level of designer. Assume one page per hour.

COST PER DESIGN
50% Productive $59.09/design
30% Productive $98.48/design

Budgeted hourly rates for creative design.

BUDGETED HOURLY RATES
Storefront
PAGE LAYOUT

INVESTMENT - Cost of computer system used	$2,500
INVESTMENT - Cost of software used	500
SPACE needed to perform this function (square feet)	20
PEOPLE - Percent of time a person is involved in activity	100%
HOURLY PAY - $15/hour	
ANNUAL HOURS (40 hrs/wk, 50 wks, 2 wks sick/vacation)	2,000

FIXED (NON VARIABLE) COSTS	@ $15/hr
Space Rent ($2.50/sq ft, 20 sq ft)	600
Depreciation (computer system, 5 yrs @ 20% per year)	500
System Insurance ($4/M of investment)	10
Basic Utilities (20%)	27
Other fixed costs ($)	10
TOTAL FIXED COSTS	1,147

VARIABLE COSTS	@ $15/hr
Wages - Direct Labor ($15/hr @ 2,080 hrs/yr)	31,200
Wages - Indirect Labor (10% of supervision required)	3,120
Pension Fund (@ 2% of labor)	686
Employee Health/Medical insurance (@$131/month)	1,572
Payroll Taxes (@11.35% of labor costs)	3,895
Workers Comp Insurance ($3/M of labor costs = 0.3%of labor costs) 103	
Task-Related added utility costs	3
Direct Supplies (taken as 1% of fixed costs and wage costs)	355
Repairs & Maintenance (@2% of hardware costs)	50
Software upgrades (@10% of investment)	50
Other variable costs	25
TOTAL VARIABLE COSTS	41,059

OTHER COSTS	
Other Misc. Costs (@10% fixed & variable costs)	4,221
SG&A Costs (overhead = 30% fixed & variable)	12,662
TOTAL OTHER COSTS	16,883

TOTAL ALL COSTS	$59,089
TOTAL HOURLY COSTS (2,000 actual hours)	$29.54/hr

COST/HOUR
- 50% Productive — 59.09/hr
- 30% Productive — 98.48/hr

UNIT OF WORK OUTPUT PER HOUR:
Newsletter — 1.34 hours/page

COST PER PAGE (NEWSLETTER)
- 50% Productive — $79.18/pg
- 30% Productive — $131.96/pg

Budgeted hourly rates for page layout.

BUDGETED HOURLY RATES
Storefront

LASER PRINTING

INVESTMENT - Cost of computer system and laser printer used	$5,000
INVESTMENT: Cost of software used	0
SPACE needed to perform this function (square feet)	20
PEOPLE - Percent of time a person is involved in activity	20%
HOURLY PAY - $7.28/hour	
ANNUAL HOURS (40 hrs/wk, 50 wks, 2 wks sick/vacation)	2,000

FIXED (NON VARIABLE) COSTS	@ $7.28/hr
Space Rent ($2.50/sq ft, 20 sq ft)	600
Depreciation (5 yrs @ 20% per year)	1,000
System Insurance ($4/M of investment)	20
Basic Utilities (20%)	27
Other fixed costs ($)	10
TOTAL FIXED COSTS	1,657

VARIABLE COSTS	@ $7.28/hr
Wages - Direct Labor ($7.28/hr @ 20% of 2,080 hrs/yr)	3,028
Wages - Indirect Labor (10% of supervision required)	303
Pension Fund (@ 2% of labor)	67
Employee Health/Medical insurance (@$131/month)	1,572
Payroll Taxes (@11.35% of labor costs)	378
Workers Comp Insurance ($3/M of labor costs)	10
Task-Related added utility costs	3
Direct Supplies (taken as 1% of fixed costs and wage costs)	50
Repairs & Maintenance (@2% of hardware costs)	50
Software upgrades (@10% of investment)	50
Other variable costs	25
TOTAL VARIABLE COSTS	5,536

OTHER COSTS	
Other Misc. Costs (@10% fixed & variable costs)	719
Sales, General & Administrative Costs (overhead = 30%)	2.158
TOTAL OTHER COSTS	2,877

TOTAL ALL COSTS	$10,070
TOTAL HOURLY COSTS (20% of actual hours)	$25.17/hr

COST/HOUR
    50% Productive $50.35/hr
    30% Productive $83.92/hr

UNIT OF WORK OUTPUT PER HOUR:
6 pages/minute, 360 pages/hour

COST PER PAGE   @ $7/hr
    50% Productive $0.14/pg
    30% Productive $0.23/pg

Budgeted hourly rates for laser printing.

The following table compares the cost baseline for a home office and a storefront business.

HOME OFFICE

OPERATION	$15/hr		$7/hr	
	50%	30%	50%	30%
Keyboarding (per page)	$4.78	$7.97	$2.40	$3.99
Scanning (per scan)	9.86	16.42	5.61	9.36
Design (per design)	47.87	79.78	-	-
Layout (per page)	64.15	106.91	-	-
Laser Printing (per pg)	0.13	0.22	0.12	0.20

STOREFRONT

OPERATION	50%	30%
Keyboarding (per page)	$3.07	$5.12
Scanning (per scan)	6.39	10.65
Design (per design)	59.09	98.48
Layout (per page)	79.18	131.96
Laser Printing (per pg)	0.14	0.23

Budgeted hourly rate comparisons for home office and storefront.

How to Use BHR to Establish Selling Price

So how do you use a budgeted hourly rate to establish selling price? Apply your baseline production standards to each specific task.

Multiply your baseline production standard by the budgeted hourly rate that you calculated for this function. Add the cost of materials and your desired profit. Then add any costs for outside services. The sum of these factors yields a total cost plus profit factor to use as the selling price.

$$\text{Selling Price} = [(\text{BHR} \times \text{Prod Std} \times \text{units})$$
$$+ \text{Material Cost}$$
$$+ \text{Other Costs} + \text{Profit}]$$

Suppose you want to set a price on providing typography services. Based on your analysis, the function "typography" has a baseline production rating of 13.2 minutes per page. This means that it takes 13.2 minutes for an average employee to setup and change the typeface, font, point size, leading, or kerning of a single column 8.5" x 11" page of 12 point type.

You have a job typesetting 10 pages of text in 12 point type, and you're to produce 300 dpi laser printed sheets for the customer. If your budgeted hourly rate for typesetting is $40 an hour, multiply 40 times the production standard (say 13.2 minutes/page), times the 10 pages all divided by 60 minutes/hour to get $88 [(40 x 13.2 x 10)/60 = 88].

Then add the costs for 10 pages of 300 dpi laser output (10 times $0.75 = $7.50) and a profit of 10 percent on both the labor and materials [(0.1 x 88) + (0.1 x 7.50) = $9.55) to yield $105.05 (88 + 7.450 + 9.55 = 105.05) for the job. Assuming there are no other costs to recover, this is what you could charge your customer. Now, what will the market bear?

As another example, suppose that you have the task to produce an eight-page newsletter. You will receive the text on typed sheets and get four graphic images to scan. The newsletter is to be printed on 8.5 x 11 paper. You are to design and layout the document, providing camera ready sheets of each page to the client. What should you charge for this effort?

First, break out all the tasks that are associated with this job. Since the text is typed, you plan to OCR scan it into the computer and then import it into the layout program.

- text scan (12 sheets of typed text, w/spellcheck)
- graphics scan (4 images w/minor cleanup)
- initial design of newsletter (8 pages, 8.5 x 11)
- layout (place text & graphics, 3 columns)
- laserset output (8 sheets, 30% graphics)

Based on your machine and operator standards, you've generated the following BHRs for these activities:

text scan	$4.89/pg	$39.12
graphics scan	$10.36 ea	82.88
design	4 hrs @ $40/hr	160.00
layout	$47.87/pg	382.96
laser print	6 min	4.00
	TOTAL BHR COSTS:	$668.96

Next add the cost of materials:

laser paper 2¢ per sheet ($0.16)
printer toner, etc. ($0.40)   = $669.52

Then add your profit (10%) and return on investment (10%):

= 669.52 + ($669.52 *0 .1) + (669.52 * 0.1)
= 669.52 + 66.95 + 66.95
= $803.42 ($100.43 per page)

This is what you could charge based on your analysis. Analyzing your market, you discover that initial newsletter design for an eight-page document with 30% graphics is running $1000. Since you are well below this, you bid $903.43 giving you $100 available for negotiation or added profit.

Quoting a flat rate is possible using BHRs, and most buyers want at least a ballpark price for the whole job rather than an hourly rate. Therefore, when asked what the job costs, study the scope of effort and give them a single price. Base it on your budgeted hourly rates and you won't go wrong.

V. Contract Standards

Writing a Good Contract

For most jobs, a written agreement doesn't seem necessary. Often a verbal agreement will bind both the customer and you for specified services. Yet there are times when a written agreement is not only necessary, it's critical.

Verbal agreements introduce a risk of misunderstanding. In addition, they tend to cover only basic issues. Contingencies may be omitted. And, verbal agreements can be difficult to enforce. A "marriage" gone sour can lead to your word against the customer's—a no-win situation.

This is why putting each agreement in writing is the best policy. The agreement that you establish between your company and your customer is critical in reducing confusion, mistrust and lost income. This contract can be a preprinted form, a custom agreement form or a purchase work order. Your customer order form is a type of contract. It should be specific enough to prevent confusion. If a dispute occurs, it becomes the reference source for resolution. A signed contract or agreement for services can be enforced legally.

Take the time to consider ever aspect of a job and address every possible thing that could be misunderstood. Deal with the who, what, where, when and how. But also deal with the scope of the job, how the final product will be delivered, what is actually provided to the customer, who own what rights, when and how payment will be made. The only requirements for a contract to exist are clearly specified terms and conditions of agreement between two parties and the signed acceptance to the agreement by both parties.

However, regardless of the form of contract or agreement that you choose to use, certain subjects should be addressed. These include a clear and detailed description of the services that you'll provide, payment schedule, what the client will deliver to you, and who owns the work when the job is complete. In addition, you should add certain statements that protect you and your company. These include indemnification, force majeure (defined in a moment), warranty disclaimer, liability limitation, governing laws, and dispute resolution.

Indemnification is protection from lawsuit based on the subject matter, composition, art or other contents of the work. Examples include copyright infringement, libel, and false or deceptive advertising claims by a third party. The contract you write must indemnify you from any responsibility for the subject matter, text, art or other contents of the publication. State that these are the sole and exclusive responsibility of the client. Have the contract state that if you are sued based on these issues, the client will pay or reimburse you for all legal costs including defense, settlement, court costs, attorney fees and losses and damages to your own business.

Force majeure refers to delays caused by actions or events beyond your control. Examples include war, strikes, storms, fire, flood, earthquake and even failures in your computer systems.

A *warranty disclaimer* is a protection to limit liability by you and your company. It points out that you make no representations or warranties regarding the services being performed other than that the services will be performed in a professional manner. The contract should state that you will not be liable for a client's lost profits or damages resulting from your performance, or failure to perform. It's also a good idea to state that your total liability to the client in any claim arising from the contract will not exeed the dollar amount that you receive from the client. In this way, a client cannot claim that you owe huge sums of money because of lost profits or lost opportunities by the client.

Governing laws are included because you may be performing services for a client who resides and operates a business outside your state. State laws can vary, and filing a suit in another state can be very expensive. I had a client who operated a testing company in California and also in Arizona. He always paid me from his Arizona office. As the work progressed, his bill grew to over $9,000. He encountered problems getting the project sold to his customer so he terminated the job and defaulted on his contract with me. When I attempted to collect the money that he owed me, my attorney explained that I had been taken by a pro. It would cost me $10,000 to recover the $9,000 because I would be forced to file suit in two states. An expensive lesson to learn.

A final paragraph that's handy to include in a contract is a statement regarding *resolution of disputes*. Since arbitration is much less expensive than the conventional legal process, insist that any dispute arising under the contract be resolved by final and binding arbitration. I say binding, because once I was trying to get a publisher to pay royalties owed me. The unethical publisher used arbitration just to determine if I could win a lawsuit against him. When it became clear that I would win, he walked out of the meeting, causing me to spend more attorney fees while he positioned himself for an out-of-court settlement. If the artibration were binding, he would have had to pay me the full amount of royalties that he was holding from me. As it was I got only 27¢ on the dollar at the final settlement meeting. My attorney earned over $7,000 and the unethical publisher walked away with about $13,000 of my royalty earnings.

This is another reason that I include in every contract a statement that, if legal action becomes necessary to secure payment, the losing party must pay all the legal fees of both parties, including payment for lost income should it be necessary for you to be away from work to handle the legal matter.

One more point about arbitration. In your contract, specify the organization that you will use for dispute resolution and where the arbitration hearings will be held (your local area is best). The American Arbitration Association is one organization you could use. There are others. Again, specify that the results of arbitration are binding on both parties.

Finally, when you have a contract written, and you feel it's a good model to use as your "standard" contract, spend the money to run the document by an attorney. The attorney can quickly determine if you've said the right things, covered the right things and provide suitable protection for you and your business.

Two thirds of your customers will just sign. The other third will use your "standard" contract as a baseline from which to negotiate.

Contracts are good for large projects, but how do you handle the everyday job—the recurring situation? Most experienced desktop providers develop some form of Terms and Conditions sheet. If included with a place for buyer and seller to sign acceptance, this is essentially a contract-on-a-page. The following section deals with Ts & Cs in detail.

Terms & Conditions

The agreement that you establish between your company and your customer is critical in reducing confusion, mistrust and lost income. The following are subjects that you should consider in developing your own terms and conditions sheet. Select and use those that best fit your type of service.

Job Estimate

This preliminary projection of costs is based upon the anticipated time to perform, prevailing labor rates, and the cost of supplies and materials. It is also a snapshot look at that point in time. State that any estimate provided the customer is not binding. It is just that—an estimate. The *quote* becomes the actual price at which you will perform work.

Order to Perform Service

The actual order to perform work can come verbally or in writing. Verbal orders and instructions should be converted to writing before you begin work on any job. Be certain to have a place for the customer to sign agreeing to the terms and conditions under which the work will be performed.

Price Quote

The fee quoted is the actual cost to the customer of services to be rendered. Your quote is based on hours of work at prevailing labor rates, the cost of supplies and materials, and services necessary to produce output. For special services beyond those specified in the agreement, state that additional charges may incur. Unless specified, quoted fees do not include preflight file conversions, editing, importing or spellchecking. But your T&C should say so.

Often meetings are required before and during a project. Your quoted fees should include expected phone consultations. You could also include customer-site consultation in your fee for orders exceeding a specified amount—say $300.

Quotes should have a time limit. Typically quotes are valid for 30 days.

Minimum Charge

Many jobs don't become profitable until a number of outputs are produced. In these cases a minimum charge is often quoted. For example, when no additional services are involved, a minimum design and layout charge of $35 could apply to any job.

Quantity Discounts

The more work, the more your resources are employed to earning profit, the better for you. Most shops offer some form of discount for multiple jobs or multiple outputs. Typically, quantity discounts apply to multiple copies of a same design. For example, scanning 12 images all 3" x 4" in size, or laser printing 50 pages of a flyer. Volume discounts vary. Study the trade catalogs and competitor price lists to determine the percentage discounted based on quantity. Then generate your own model and publish this in your own counter price book. You could give 5% off for handling 15 to 30 pieces, 10% off for up to 100 and 15% off for over 100 of each.

Quantity discounts can also apply to the number of jobs that a client brings to you. For example, a client is planning to produce 10 different saddle-stitch brochures, all the same size. You want the job to design and produce all ten, so you offer a discounted price to the client if they agree to give you the complete 10-brochure project. Then bill each individual brochure at the discounted rate.

Additional Charges

Specify in your counter price book when additional charges apply. For example, you could provide film output at 2070 dpi, but charge 50% more if the output is 3000 dpi or greater.

Charge for placing scans, fixing files, and customer alterations. If the customer gives you a laser proof on an imagesetting job, apply a surcharge if the disk file is not provided or if the proof is not marked with a color break.

Specify the type of paper used for your laser output. Charge more if a different paper, or a higher resolution is requested.

Customers sometimes ask you to perform services for which you have no resources. You could offer to use outside services (where you become the broker). Indicate those additional services that could be brokered out. Provide an estimate of the additonal cost to the customer. Until they become familiar with the process, most customers will prefer that you coordinate the added work for them. This can increase your total income from a job. It could also help you develop job-sharing with other businesses. However, state that you are not liable for output errors, conflicts or delays caused by other businesses.

What Customer Must Provide

Usually a customer brings in a draft drawing, a computer file or a laser proof. If you are to imageset the job, be certain to specify that ALL font families used to produce the disk file are listed and given to you. For example you could indicate that a customer's failure to list all font families could result in improper billable output, that fonts other than Adobe or Linotype must be supplied. Also specify if there is a download charge per font. For example, if pages are output with bitmapped fonts because the fonts were not listed, the customer should be charged for the redo.

Specify the image format for all scans (CGM, EPS, GIF, PCX, PICT, or TIFF, PC or Mac).

Hold the customer responsible for the content, construction and accuracy of all materials turned over to you. This includes trapping of all files.

Time to Perform

Outputs that take longer than 10 minutes to RIP should be charged at the shop hourly rate in 10 minute increments. Some companies apply a surcharge if a file required more than 15 minutes to complete. The same goes for color proof output. Pages with heavy ink or toner coverage take longer to produce and use more materials. Thus you should charge more when more raw materials are used in the process.

Who Has Rights to Output?

Copyright and ownership have been discussed and debated for years. The law says that the originator of a work holds copyright unless it is released to another in writing. If you use clip art in a work, do you have the right to alter the clip art and claim ownership yourself? Most stock houses say that if you purchase an image for a specific use, you have the right to use the image for that use. But major alterations to an image must be negotiated with the original owner of the image. Some images can be purchased royalty-free—you can use them in anything that you're selling. You just can't resell the images themselves. But read the licensing agreement or contract carefully, and call the image clip art vendor to resolve any questions. Some vendors who sell royalty-free images for multimedia and electronic presentations still vary in their treatment of when and how these images can be used. For example, one CD clip art vendor gives you a 10,000 copy free use of each image. After that, they apply a one-time fee for additional copies.

It's best to work out an understanding on rights before work proceeds. I usually hire freelance work on a "work for hire" basis. This means that whatever they produce is owned by me and I hold copyright. You may want to hold copyright to work that you produce for others—especially if you think they may use your work in other applications.

Some Ts&Cs point out that all original materials are protected by copyright but are released to the customer upon final payment for a project.

If you develop stock photographs or stock clip art and sell these to a client, you must decide up front what rights go with the Work. Typically, commercial stock houses consider the use of images for print or multimedia in the same manner. The seller determines if the Work is for one-time use or unlimited use.

State that working computer files, mechanical art and film assembled for production by your employees remain the property of your shop.

Electronic Rights

Electronic rights include (but are not limited to) the right to reproduce all of a Work in any form of data storage that is portable including magnetic disks, CD-ROM discs, and streaming tapes. And it covers the right to enter the Work in a computer database or network.

Specify in your Agreement how the product of your services will be used. If the customer decides to use your Work in another application, you may be due added compensation.

Form of Delivery

You must clearly specify what will be provided to the customer. Will you turn over hard copy and a disk? Will it be a proof with the film? Determine this and then put it in writing so no confusion occurs.

On color laser output, have the customer indicate if a file can be tiled or reduced if the image area exceeds a specified size (e.g., 8 x 9 for letter size or 8 x 12 for legal size).

Paper Output: Specify how all files will be printed, at what size and line screen. Also specify if it will be right-reading paper with crop marks.

Film Output: Specify if output is right-reading, emulsion-down composite with the same defaults as for paper, or specify what output is required.

Number of Copies Provided

Usually one final print, proof or image file is provided. In the case of resumes, often an original is provided with several reprints that the client can use. Some shops include blank sheets of similar paper and matching envelopes with each resume job. The blank sheets are used to generate a cover letter for the resume. Specify up front how many copies will be provided.

Disks/Tape Media Delivered With Hard Copy

Files are usually held by the service provider for a set time period—say six months. After that they are sold to the customer for the cost of the media or destroyed. Unique projects are usually kept by the service provider for use as idea-generators in other applications. Just be certain you don't violate the customer's copyright.

Also require that the customer have a back-up file on all work submitted to you. Accept files only if they are not the customer's master file. In your Agreement, limit the liability for loss of any material turned over to you, to the replacement costs of the media only.

Alterations by Client

Changes to a customer's file directed by the customer should be billed at the shop's hourly rate.

Cancellation and Job Interruptions

You need to cover yourself should your client terminate a job after you've already started. State in your agreement that a work order can be cancelled only after you are compensated for all work performed and materials used to date on that job. In addition, require compensation for any work related obligations that you enter into regarding that order. For example:

"If your job is in production and you cancel the order, a minimum of $30 will be charged plus any additional costs that we've incurred depending on how far the order has progressed."

Cover yourself for contingencies. State that all work orders are accepted subject to strikes, floods, fires, earthquakes, vandalism, acts of God, and any other work stoppage beyond your control. Hold yourself and your company harmless for work delays or stoppage that you can't control.

Layouts, Dummies and Paste-Ups

Here's how to handle these:

"Services to produce a preliminary representation of a job accumulate charges at prevailing rates. No use shall be made of, or ideas taken from, such preliminary work without the expressed permission of our shop and only upon payment of just compensation by you, the customer."

Acceptance of Proofs

Guarantee the accuracy of your work. Correct any errors and omissions at no charge. Then produce a composite proof for the client. Insist that they sign or mark OK on an approval form before work can begin. Once the customer accepts a proof output, any customer-directed changes made after this point are billed to the client.

Standard of Quality

Establish what acceptance criteria will be used to gauge quality. Then hold yourself and the customer to this.

Guaranteed Satisfaction

If a customer is not satisfied with the work, offer to do the work again as long as nothing in the scope of the job changes.

If a customer is not satisfied, they can terminate the project at any time and owe only for the work completed to that moment. Or let them cancel the contract without further obligation to pay the remaining monies agreed in writing.

Specify that the product that you produce for your client is supplied on an "as is" basis. State that your company does not warrant the merchantability of its services or products or guarantee or make any representation regarding the suitability of any customer directed product for any particular use or application.

Rush Rates

Most jobs are scheduled and delivered in one day (24 hours from time of acceptance). In fact, most price lists specify that the normal turnaround time on output jobs is 24 hours. Turnaround time should begin when the job arrives at your shop. This time depends on the complexity of the files, the size of the job and your own work load.

A premium is charged for producing output sooner because this disrupts the normal flow of work and impacts good scheduling practices. You should be paid additional when the urgency of their job forces you to stop production on an existing job. Publish your standard and rush turnaround times and rates. Here's an example:

Normal Rate:
    24-hour turnaround (bill at 100% price listed)

Express Rate:
    under 24 hours add 25% (bill at 125% of price listed)

Priority Rate:
    under 4 hours add 50% (bill at 150% of price listed)

After Hours Rate:
    add 75% (bill at 175% of price listed)

While You Wait:
    add 100% surcharge (bill at 200% of price listed)

Overtime

If a customer asks you to have someone work in excess of your prevailing regular daily schedule of hours, charge overtime at the prevailing rate in your area—typically billed at time and a half, double time on weekends or holidays.

Shipping & Handling

Preparing the work for transportation or mailing has a cost. Be certain that the client understands that they will be charged the prevailing rate for shipping and handling. For example, a box, packing, tape and label has a cost. So does the time to fill and seal the box. You should be paid for time and materials on this added work.

Delivery

Specify if delivery is to the billing address, another location, or if the customer will pick up the job at your shop. Delivery is the conveying of work to a point designated by the customer, or upon deposit of the work with a common carrier (UPS, FedEx, Airborne, etc.) or with the U.S. Postal Service. State that your company assumes no responsibility after "delivery" has occurred.

Indemnification

State that your company will not be liable for direct, indirect, incidental or consequential costs including damages for related losses, due to your company's use or inability to use any software. Have the customer sign a statement that the customer will indemnify and hold your company harmless for any and all claims arising from submitting work to you.

Lien

A lien is a right to hold propery of another pending payment of an outstanding debt. State that you have the right under the ageement to retain all materials or property belonging to the customer, as well as any work that has been performed, until all just claims against the client are satisfied. You hold everything as a security deposit, releasing the job to them upon payment or acceptable payment terms.

Billing Procedure / Getting Paid

The agreement that you establish between your company and your customer is critical in reducing confusion, mistrust and lost income. Here are some thoughts regarding payment.

Non-contract work is payable upon delivery. Contract fees may be paid in installments if agreed before work proceeds. For C.O.D. orders, you could require a 50% deposit on the job.

If the work involves printing, be aware that most printers require payment of half of a job up front and payment on the remainder upon delivery. If you subcontract the printing ,get up-front payment from your customer. You are not a bank and cannot afford to carry the cash flow for your client. The concept is simple. You get paid, you pay the subcontractor, everyone wins.

For large projects, one third payment is due upon signing agreement for the work; one third is due upon delivery of first draft (or first proof), and the final third is due upon delivery of the completed project.

Work is billed on the basis of work completed. If a client cancels a job, all billable work performed to that point will be due and payable.

Invoiced work is payable and due 30 days from the date of the invoice. If you get a rubber check, charge a penalty fee for running it through the bank processing again. Typical penalty charge for returned checks: $15 - $20. On your invoices, print a statement that if the client is late in paying the invoice, a late fee applies — often 1.5% per month or any portion of a month.

If legal action is required to collect on an invoice, specify on your Agreement that the purchaser agrees to pay all costs, including reasonable attorney fees associated with the collection on any delinquent account.

For orders delivered to foreign customers, specify that payment will be in U.S. dollars and must include foreign shipping charges. Most credit card companies handle this for you automatically if the charge is applied within the U.S.

Taxes

State that your prices are exclusive of any Federal, State, or Local sales, use, or excise taxes levied upon, or measured by the sale or use of goods required in the performance of this contract. Then be certain to list any taxes that apply to the transaction. In most cases, taxes are appropriate on service work. Your state tax board can help you determine when and how to levy a sales tax on any type work that you do.

If a customer is buying your products or services for resale, get a copy of their resale license number and mark this on the invoice. Plan early to clear an audit.

Insolvency of Buyer

If a client becomes bankrupt or insolvent during the term of a contract, state in your Agreement that the contract may be terminated without prejudice to your right to collect any amounts then due or affect any other rights that you may have under the law.

Get a Signature

It's important that your customer be made aware of the terms and conditions under which each job will be performed. Take the time to go over your T&C page with them before you begin. Then have them sign the work order (usually on the side containing the terms and conditions) so both you and they know the rules of the game.

VI. Glossary of Definitions

The following definitions are provided to establish a common baseline for analysis and standards generation.

alteration - addition, change or modification to the copy, style or specifications of work made by a customer.

average type - light to medium type coverage with one or two fonts type complexity on page. Simple line art graphics may be included at no extra charge. Examples include basic forms and typical newsletter pages.

burden rate - some shops calculate overhead by combining both direct and indirect costs (total annual expense). Then they convert this overhead into a burden rate by subtracting direct labor from the total annual expense and dividing this result by the direct labor expense. Burden rate can exceed 200% of costs.

burdened hourly rate - result of adding the burden rate to the hourly fee. This means that each employee has a portion of overhead allocated to their billable work whenever they bid a job. Large companies often use accounting systems that apply the burden rate concept.

buy-outs , job-outs - subcontracting tasks not within the scope of your capabilities. Many shops mark up subcontractor charges 30-50% to arrive at the selling price to quote their customers.

chance order - speculation of an order; producing work without charge in expectation of getting the order.

comp - reproduction of composition, graphic or illustration to show final appearance. Also called *proof,* or *rough.*

correction - change in the composition or other work performed by your business due to errors made by your or your staff; usually made without charge.

custom graphics - complex illustrations, display type and rules involving heavy design and manipulation. Examples include logos, logotype and customer-directed graphics. Clip art is considered simple graphics since only importing is involved.

debt servicing - making payments on a loan to buy equipment. When you break out your machine and labor costs, remember the overhead allocated to the costs of your equipment. If you're making payments on hardware, you should allocate this cost over the hours that the hardware will be used.

direct costs - expenses directly related to a job or project. These costs can be associated with a unique project number or work order.

estimate - preliminary projection of costs; not intended to be binding (a quote does this).

fixed costs - those expenses that you must pay whether you have little or lots of business. Fixed costs don't vary with the volume of sales. They exist just because you're in business.

general and administrative (G&A.) - expenses that include secretarial support, clerical help, and any cost not covered under direct and indirect labor or manufacturing costs.

heavy page composition - heavy type coverage with solid straight 8-point type. Closely spaced cross rule form with multiple borders or box heads. Examples include the fine print in Terms & Conditions.

indirect costs - those expenses that can not be directly charged to a specific job or project. These costs become overhead expenses to your business. Indirect costs can include both fixed and variable costs.

layout/paste-up - preliminary representation of work created as a prototype for production.

light page composition - light to medium type coverage with one or two font sizes on page. Open spaced cross rule form with minimal borders. Examples include basic 12-line announcement flyer.

machine standard - performance baseline based on the capability of your hardware and software.

medium page composition - medium type coverage with solid straight 10-point type. Normal spaced cross rule form with simple borders or box heads. For example: a book interior page.

non-proportional type - each letter occupies the same amount of line space regardless of its width.

overhead costs - the indirect expenses that we must pay whether or not we sell a product or service. Overhead costs do not necessarily include designer and technician wages.

overhead factor - result of dividing the hourly overhead by your hourly income. This is how much of your hourly labor rate is allocated to paying for overhead.

preliminary proof - reproduction of composition, graphic or illustration to show final appearance. Also called *comp, proof,* or *rough.*

production standard - how much time it takes to complete a task or to produce a product. The production standard incorporates the human aspect of a job. It helps you determine the typical times to perform billable shop activities.

quotation (quote) - statement of price for performing specified work.

rough - reproduction of composition, graphic or illustration to show final appearance. Also called *proof,* or *comp.*

selling, general and administrative (SG&A) - composite benchmark combining selling costs with general and administrative costs. SG&A can vary from company to company and from industry to industry. It can include travel expenses, copying services, consumable supplies, and possibly sales overhead costs. Because its comption varies, it's difficult to compare SG&A values among companies.

simple graphics - easily produced with minimal manipulation; illustrations, display type and rules used to enhance look of a document. Examples include rounded boxes and clip art.

standard typing output - 70 words per minute (about 4 pages per hour) with good English and grammar.

proportional type - each letter occupies a different amount of line space. For example, a "w" takes up more space than the letter "I" in proportional type. Overall, about 30% more text can fit on a page using proportional type.

terms - conditions of a sale.

type intensive - heavy type coverage. Examples include forms, difficult tables, and many-word menus.

variable costs - those expenses that change with the level of business activity.

very heavy page composition - extra heavy type coverage with 6 point type in complicated arrangement. Closely spaced cross rule form with complex borders or box heads. Examples include Terms & Conditions and other "fine print" pages.

very light page composition - light type coverage with one or two fonts on page. Very open spaced cross rule form with no borders. Examples include basic 7-line announcement flyer.

Index

Brenner Information Group
P.O. Box 721000, San Diego, CA 92172-1000
ORDERS: (800) 811-4337   fax: (619) 484-2599

Order Form   www.brennerbooks.com

Date: _______________

Name: ____

Company: ____

Address: ____

____

City: ____

State/Province: _________________ ZIP/Mail Postal Code _____________

Telephone: ( ) _________________________ Country: _____________

Fax: ( ) _________________________

SHIP TO: ____

____

HOW YOU FOUND US:

QTY	ITEM	EACH	PRICE	TOTAL
____	BRENNER BUNDLE	$99.95	____	____
____	Language of Computer Publishing	$24.95	____	____
____	Pricing Guide for Desktop Services	$34.95	____	____
____	Pricing Guide for Web Services	$29.95	____	____
____	Pricing Tables: Desktop Services	$49.95	____	____
	Small Indep Publisher Report	$50.00		

PRIORITY SHIPPING

Quantity	U.S.	Canada	Other Countries
1 book	$5	$7	$15
2 books	$6	$10	$28
3 books	$7	$12	$34
More	(CALL)	(CALL)	(CALL)

Sub-Total ____________

Sales Tax (CA buyers) ____________

Shipping

TOTAL (U.S. funds)

PAYMENT: CHECK (Make check out to BRENNER INFORMATION GROUP)

CREDIT CARD (*VISA, Mastercard, Discover Card, Diners Club*)

CREDIT CARD INFORMATION:

Card #: ____

Expiration Date: _______________________

Name on the card: ________________________________

Signature: ____

Thank You For The Order!

Desktop Production Standards Software Templates

Spreadsheets for Business Success

The following is a description of 16 spreadsheet modules provided with the reference book *Desktop Production Standards*.

These spreadsheets are designed to help you develop your own timing standards. You must have Microsoft® Excel version 5.0 (Mac or PC) to open and use these worksheets, although some other spreadsheet programs will open and translate Excel files to their native file language.

MACHINE STANDARDS

Scanning (Line Art, Grayscale, Photographs)

Calculates average scan rate.

Inputs: Start-up or Set-up time in minutes and seconds.

Image size being scanned (in square inches).

Resolution of scan.

Start and finish times.

Output: Scan Rate in minutes per square inch.

Average Start-Up/Set-Up Time in minutes.

Average Image Size in square inches.

Average Scan Resolution.

Average Scan Rate in minutes per sq. inch.

Scanning - OCR

Calculates average scan rate per page.

Inputs: Start-up or Set-up time in minutes and seconds.

Image text area being scanned (in square inches).

Resolution of scan.

Scan rate first page (in seconds).

Scan rate next page (in seconds).

Output: Average Start-Up/Set-Up Time in minutes.

Average Text Image Size in square inches.

Average Scan Resolution.

Average Scan Page Rate in seconds.

Printing (Thermal, Inkjet, Laser, Imagesetter)

Calculates average printing time for thermal, inkjet, laser printers based on three levels of complexity (text only, 30% art, and 70% art).

Inputs: Printing time at specific complexity (in seconds)

Output: Total Number of Pages (each complexity)

Total Print Time (each complexity)

Average Print Time (each complexity)

OPERATOR TIMING STANDARDS

Keyboarding

Calculates characters entered per page, the total time, the characters entered per minute on each project task and then the results for each of three levels of complexity—total number of jobs, total character per minute entered and the average characters per minute keyboarded.

Inputs: Hardware and Software Used

Project Task

Time Start and End

Difficulty Level (low, medium, high)

Number of Words Entered

Number of Characters Entered

Number of Pages Entered

Output: Characters per Page
               Total Time per Project Task
               Characters per Minute
               Total Number of Jobs (each level of difficulty)
               Total Characters per Minute
               Average Characters per Minute (by difficulty)

Typography

Calculates pages per hour and characters per hour for typographic design. Also calculates the average pages set up per hour and the average hours per page.

Inputs: Hardware and Software Used
        In What Form Work Was Submitted
        Project Description
        Initial Page Count
        Final Page Count
        Start/End Times
        Typefaces Used
        Number of Point Sizes Used
        Number of Characters Set
        Number of Words Set

Output: Total Time
               Pages Set per Hour
               Characters Set per Hour
               Total Pages Completed
               Average Pages Set per Hour
               Average Hours per Page Set

Page Layout

Calculates total pages laid out, total time expended and the average hours per page laid out at each of three different complexity levels — text only, 30% art, and 70% art.

Inputs: Hardware and Software Used
        Project Description
        Start and Finish Dates
        Complexity of each page
        Start and Finish Time (each page)

Output: Total Time (each page)
Total Pages (each complexity level)
Average Hours per Page

Scan Retouch

Calculates total retouch jobs at each of three complexity levels —simple, average and difficult. Also calculates the total work time and average time to retouch a scan at each complexity level.

Inputs: Hardware and Software Used
Project Description
File Type and Name
Scan Size (in square inches)
Start-Up / Set-Up Time (in minutes)
Complexity of Job Session
Start and Finish Time

Outputs: Total Time (each session)
Total Number of Jobs (each complexity)
Average Time (minutes and seconds) at each complexity level

Color Editing

Calculates total color editing jobs at each of three complexity levels —simple, average and difficult. Also calculates the total work time and average time to edit an image at each complexity level.

Inputs: Hardware and Software Used
Project Description
File Type and Name
Start-Up / Set-Up Time (in minutes)
Complexity of Job Session
Start and Finish Time

Outputs: Total Time (each session)
Total Number of Jobs (each complexity)
Average Time (minutes and seconds) at each complexity level

Cost & Overhead Analyzer

Calculates total fixed and variable costs, monthly overhead and a running average of the monthly overhead for a full year. After entering the hours worked each month, the worksheet calculates the hourly overhead and the average hourly overhead for each month. At the far right of the spreadsheet, one column contains the cumulative cost for each category and an adjacent column contains the percentage that each cost category is of the total annual costs.

Inputs: Year of Analysis

    Actual Cost Data

    Actual Hours Worked Each Month

Outputs: Total Fixed Costs

    Total Variable Costs

    Monthly Overhead

    Average Monthly Overhead to Date

    Hourly Overhead

    Average Hourly Overhead to Date

    Annual Cumulative Cost (each category)

    Percent of Total Cost (each category)

    Total Hours Worked to Date

BUDGETED HOURLY RATE COSTS

Budgeted Hourly Rates (Keyboarding, Design, Scanning, Lasersetting, Open Form)

Calculates budgeted cost per hour for any task performed by a shop. Enables analyzer to enter basis information including margin of safety, sales, general and administrative overhead, and productivity. To the BHR result, an estimator can add cost of materials, profit, and return on investment to establish a "could charge" price. Then by knowing what the market is charging, the owner can set the hourly rate somewhere between "could charge" and "market is charging."

Inputs: Preparation Date

     Cost of Equipment Used

     Cost of Software Used

     Space Required to Perform Work (square feet)

     Percent of Available Time Needed

     Hourly Pay of Person Doing Work

     Actual Hours Worked (Annually)

     Total Hours Paid (Yearly)

     Rent (monthly, per square foot)

     Depreciation (percent of annual costs)

     Insurance (premium per $1,000 of equip cost)

     Utility Costs (basic monthly rate)

     Other Fixed Costs

     Direct Labor Wages

     Indirect Wages (percent of supervisor time)

     Pension Deduction (percent of wages)

     Employee Insurance (monthly cost for life, health, medical, vision, dental, etc.)

     Payroll Taxes (percent of wages applied to social security, unemployment and state disability taxes)

     Workers Compensation Insurance (premium per $1,000 of payroll cost)

     Task-Specific Utility Cost (annual dollars in added utility cost for this task)

     Direct Supplies (percent of fixed costs and wage costs)

     Repair & Maintenance (percent of equipment costs)

     Software Upgrades (percent of software cost)

     Other Variable Costs

     Miscellaneous Costs (percent of total fixed and variable costs reserved as margin of safety)

     SG&A (percent of overhead associated with sales, general and administrative costs

     Shop Productivity

     Unit of Work Output per Hour

Outputs: Rent Cost (in dollars)
                  Depreciation (in dollars)
                  Insurance Costs (in dollars)
                  Utility Costs (annual cost based on percent of
                      space used)
                  Total All Fixed Costs
                  Direct Labor Costs (in dollars, based on
                      hourly pay times hours worked per year)
                  Indirect Wages (dollars of indirect labor
                      added for supervision)
                  Pension Fund (in dollars, typically 1-3% of
                      payroll)
                  Employee Insurance, Payroll Taxes and
                      Workers Comp Costs (in dollars)
                  Direct Supplies (in dollars)
                  Repairs and Maintenance (in dollars)
                  Software Upgrade Reserve (in dollars)
                  Other Variable Costs
                  Total All Variable Costs
                  Margin of Safety Reserve (in dollars)
                  SG&A Costs (in dollars)
                  Annual Total Costs (this task)
                  Total Hourly Costs (this task)
                  BHR Cost per Hour (in dollars, based on shop
                      productivity)
                  Cost per Unit of Work

######

ENTERING DATA:

Each worksheet has a color background with entry cells in white boxes. Enter data into each white box. The results are automatically calculated and presented in the results boxes or columns.

<u>PRINTING A MODULE:</u>

It's best to select (highlight) the module that you want to print and then print in black and white. On color printers select "No Color" or "Black & White" before commanding the computer to print. This removes the color background and prints the module spreadsheet in black on white paper.

RESTARTING WITH CLEAN WORKSHEET

Save completed worksheet with new name. Copy clean, unused spreadsheet from Master disk into hard disk (over-writing old data on original file). Your completed archive data is stored with the new name. For example. save *costanal.xls* as *costDec98.xls*. Then load *costanal.xls* from master disk, overwriting old *costanal.xls file*. You now have two files: one clean *costanal.xls* and an archive *costDec98.xls*.

Other Products
Pricing Guide for Desktop Services
Pricing Guide for Web Services
Pricing Tables: Desktop Services
Language of Computer Publishing

FOR COMPLETE DESCRIPTIONS
(including table of contents and testimonials)

www.brennerbooks.com